Aloha
IN EVERY BITE
HOLIDAY EDITION

R.J. Pickrell

Wordsmiths, Ink LLC

Copyright © 2025 R.J. Pickrell

All rights reserved. No part of this publication may be reproduced, distributed, or transmitted in any form or by any means, electronic, mechanical, photocopying, recording, or otherwise, without the prior written permission of the publisher, except in the case of brief quotations used in reviews or critical articles.

Published by Wordsmiths, Ink, Gilbert, AZ
Wordsmiths, Ink LLC

For information, contact: **info@AlohainEveryBite.com**
Visit: **www.AlohainEveryBite.com**

ISBN: 978-1-970960-02-0
First Edition
Printed in the USA

This is a work of culinary nonfiction. While recipes, techniques, and commentary are based on the author's personal experience and expertise, any references to individuals, restaurants, or products are included for informational purposes only. Any resemblance to actual persons, living or dead, is purely coincidental unless otherwise stated.

The author and publisher disclaim any liability for adverse reactions to the use of the recipes or misuse of the ingredients or techniques described herein.

Cover design by: R.J. Pickrell
Food photography by: R.J. Pickrell
Edited by: R.J. Pickrell
Cover image copyright © 2025 R.J. Pickrell

Table of Contents

Welcome/About Us	1
Meet the Flavors of Paia Spice Co.	2-3
How Hawaii Celebrates Western Holidays	4-7
Holiday Food History in Hawai'i	8-11
Ancestral & Modern Holiday Rituals	12-15
Thanksgiving Recipes	16-37
Christmas Recipes	38-59
New Years Recipes	60-80

Welcome to Paia Spice Co.

Welcome to Paia Spice Co., where Aloha meets bold, unforgettable flavor. Whether you're grilling beachside or cooking at home, our handcrafted seasonings and salts are made to elevate every dish with the vibrant spirit of Maui. Mahalo for bringing "Aloha for Your Food" into your kitchen!

Our Story: Born in Maui

On Maui, the best gifts are Aloha and a great meal.

When Jen and I moved to Maui, we quickly learned that food was one of the best ways to connect with others. One day, while experimenting in the kitchen, I accidentally combined two spices that weren't meant to go together, but the result was magic. That happy accident became Big Haole's Original All-Purpose Seasoning.

At first, we gave our blends away. But the demand kept growing. With the help of our neighbor Kaleo, who started selling our seasonings to surfers at Hoʻokipa Beach Park, Paia Spice Co. became a reality.

Over time, we developed more blends—each taking about six months to perfect. Our goal has always been the same: craft bold, aromatic flavors you can't find in stores, using generous herbs and spices. All while staying true to our mission of being "The Local Spice at a Local Price." Thank you for supporting our dream and sharing the gift of Aloha with every meal.

Jen & Big Haole

Meet the Flavors

Aunty Jen's Seasonings

Aunty Jen's Caribbean Seasoning

A tropical blend of 16 warm spices that deliver bold island flavor without overpowering heat. Ideal for pork, chicken, beef, vegetables, and more, this savory mix adds depth with just a hint of kick.

Aunty Jen's Greek Seasoning

A Mediterranean, inspired all-purpose blend with 12 herbs and spices. Perfect on chicken, lamb, pork, veggies, soups, and of course, a classic Greek salad.

Aunty Jen's Pizza & Things Seasoning

This Italian herb packed blend delivers more flavor and aroma than typical pizza seasonings. Great on pizza, pasta, garlic bread, lasagna, and any dish needing a savory Italian twist.

Aunty Jen's Hela Wela Seasoning

Our hottest blend yet; crafted with habanero heat, Kiawe smoke, and bold island flavor. The spice builds slowly, enhancing food without overwhelming it. Try it on tropical fruits, tacos, brunch, or BBQ.

Big Haole's Seasonings

Big Haole's Blackened Seasoning

A smoky, citrusy twist on traditional blackened seasoning with a touch of lemon basil. Great on fish, chicken, tacos, and even chicken salad for a flavorful punch.

Big Haole's Kiawe Seasoning

Infused with natural Kiawe smoke, this all-purpose blend is ideal for steaks, seafood, veggies, and even Bloody Mary rims. A smoky, savory must-have for your spice shelf.

Big Haole's Original Seasoning

Our signature all-purpose blend that started it all. Goes great on everything, meats, veggies, soups, eggs, rice, even popcorn. A true everyday seasoning for kitchen and grill.

Big Haole's Pika Seasoning

"Pika" means spicy in Hawaiian, and this blend brings the heat! A spicier version of Original, it's perfect for wings, fries, pastas, and those who like a little fire in their food.

Meet the Flavors
Hawaiian Salts

Bamboo Jade Pa'akai
Infused with bamboo leaf extract, this vibrant green salt adds an earthy umami flavor and a stunning finish to seafood, grilled meats, vegetables, and more.

Black Lava Pa'akai
Striking black sea salt blended with activated coconut charcoal. Adds smoky flair and detox benefits, ideal for seafood, salads, fruits, and as a dramatic finishing salt.

Kiawe Smoked Sea Salt
Smoked with native Kiawe wood, this bold, aromatic salt brings authentic Hawaiian BBQ flavor to meats, stews, veggies, and marinades.

Red 'Alaea Pa'akai
Traditional Hawaiian sea salt enriched with volcanic clay. Deep red, mineral-rich, and perfect for kalua pork, poke, and other island classics, or as a finishing touch on any dish.

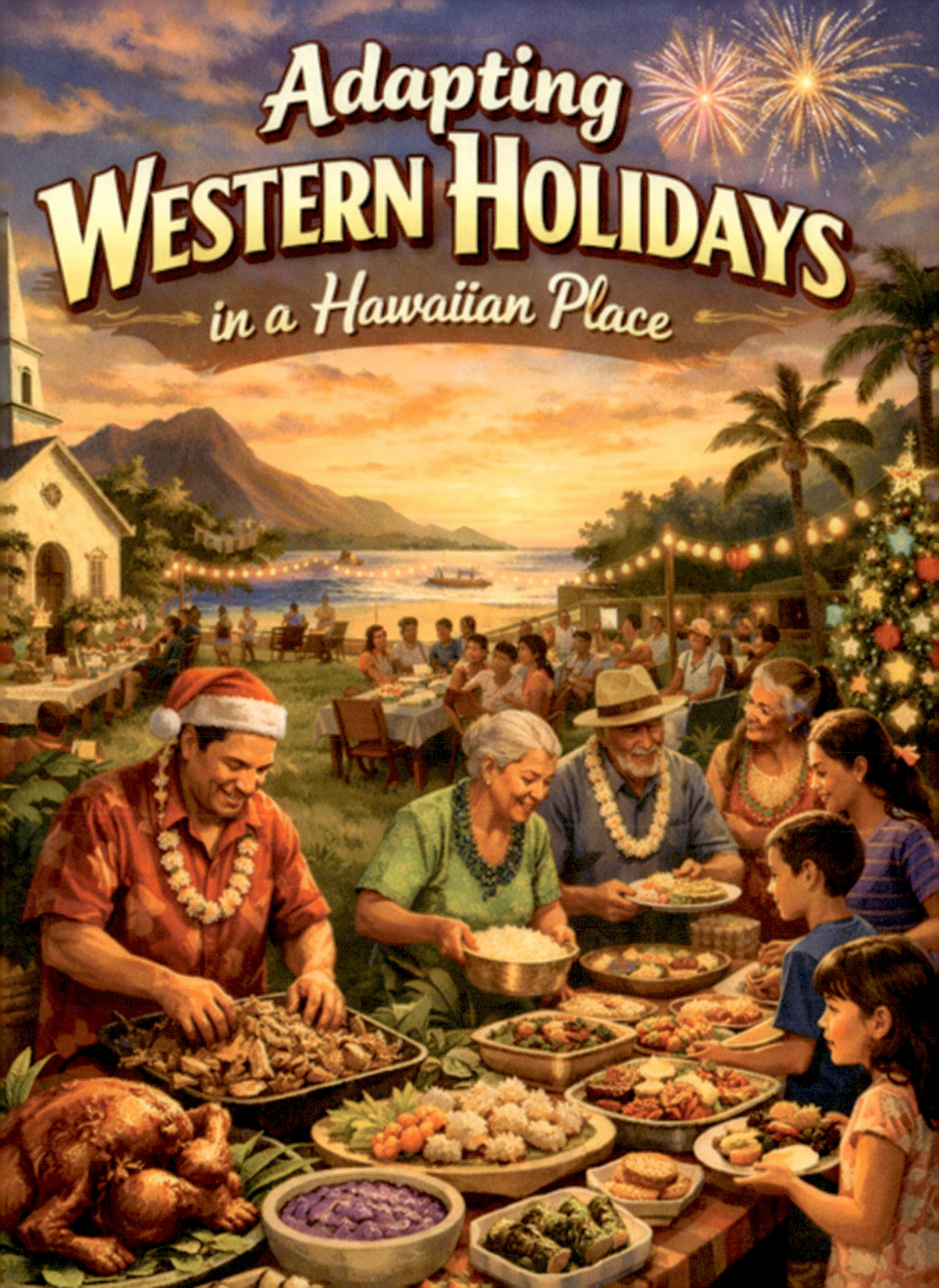

How Hawai'i Celebrates "Western" Holidays

In Hawai'i, holidays such as Christmas, Thanksgiving, and New Year's did not arrive as blank slates. They came layered with foreign customs, Christian traditions, and Western calendars, but they were not simply adopted. They were **reshaped**, absorbed into existing ways of gathering, feeding community, and honoring 'ohana. Rather than replacing Hawaiian values, these holidays became new occasions to practice them.

Adapting Western Holidays in a Hawaiian Place

When Christmas and Thanksgiving were introduced through missionaries and later reinforced during the plantation era, they arrived with familiar mainland symbols: roasted meats, formal table settings, and church-centered observances. But Hawai'i is not a place of cold winters or isolated nuclear families. It is a place of **shared labor, outdoor living, extended 'ohana, and communal meals.**

As a result, holidays evolved to reflect island life.
- Meals moved outdoors.
- Formal courses gave way to shared tables.
- Imported traditions were softened by local ingredients, flavors, and rhythms.

What emerged was not imitation, but **local expression.**

Missionary Influence vs. Local Reinterpretation

Christian missionaries brought Christmas observances, hymns, and church gatherings in the 19th century. Over time, these practices blended with Hawaiian concepts of celebration rather than overtaking them.

While church services became part of holiday observance for many families, the **center of celebration remained the meal,** not as ceremony, but as relationship.

Local families adapted holidays in ways that made sense:
- Food was prepared collectively.
- Recipes were adjusted to what was available.
- Celebration emphasized abundance and sharing, not formality.

Rather than a single "correct" way to celebrate, holidays became flexible shaped by family, island, and generation.

Why Hawaiian Holiday Tables Look Different

A Hawaiian holiday table often looks less like a formal dining spread and more like a lū'au without protocol. This reflects several realities:
- Large, multi-generational gatherings
- Outdoor cooking traditions
- A preference for shared dishes over plated meals
- The influence of plantation-era potlucks

Food is meant to be passed, not presented.
You will often see:
- Poi alongside turkey
- Rice instead of stuffing
- Multiple interpretations of the same dish
- Desserts made by many hands, not one host

This table is not curated, it is collective.

The Rise of the Lū'au-Style Christmas Meal
Over time, Christmas meals in Hawai'i shifted away from formal roasts and toward something more familiar: lū'au-style abundance.

Rather than a single centerpiece, the table expanded:
- Multiple proteins
- Steamed and slow-cooked dishes
- Foods that could feed many without strict timing

This style of eating mirrors traditional gatherings, where food is plentiful, flexible, and meant to last all day.

Christmas became less about the spectacle of a meal and more about the continuity of gathering.

Why Kalua Turkey Replaced Ham
Kalua cooking methods, slow-cooked, smoky, deeply seasoned—fit both Hawaiian taste and large gatherings.

Turkey, introduced as a holiday staple through Western influence, adapted easily:
- It could be cooked underground or in ovens mimicking imu techniques
- It fed many people
- Its flavor paired well with poi, rice, and gravy

Ham, while still present, never fully replaced the role of slow, cooked, shared meats. Kalua turkey became a bridge, honoring introduced holidays while maintaining local cooking identity.

How Potlucks Shaped Modern Hawaiian Celebrations
Plantation life shaped how holidays functioned in Hawai'i more than formal traditions ever could.

With diverse communities, limited resources, and large families, potlucks became essential. No single household carried the burden of feeding everyone. Each person brought what they could, and together, there was abundance.

This practice continues today.
Holiday meals are often:
- Organized informally
- Shared across families and neighbors
- A mix of traditional, modern, and personal dishes

The potluck is not a shortcut; it is an expression of kōkua and shared responsibility.

Celebration as Continuity
In Hawai'i, holidays are not rigid reenactments of imported customs. They are living gatherings, shaped by place, people, and memory.

Christmas, Thanksgiving, and New Years are less about what the calendar dictates and more about what the table holds:
- Time together
- Food prepared with intention
- The continuation of 'ohana traditions—old and new

This is the spirit carried into the recipes that follow.

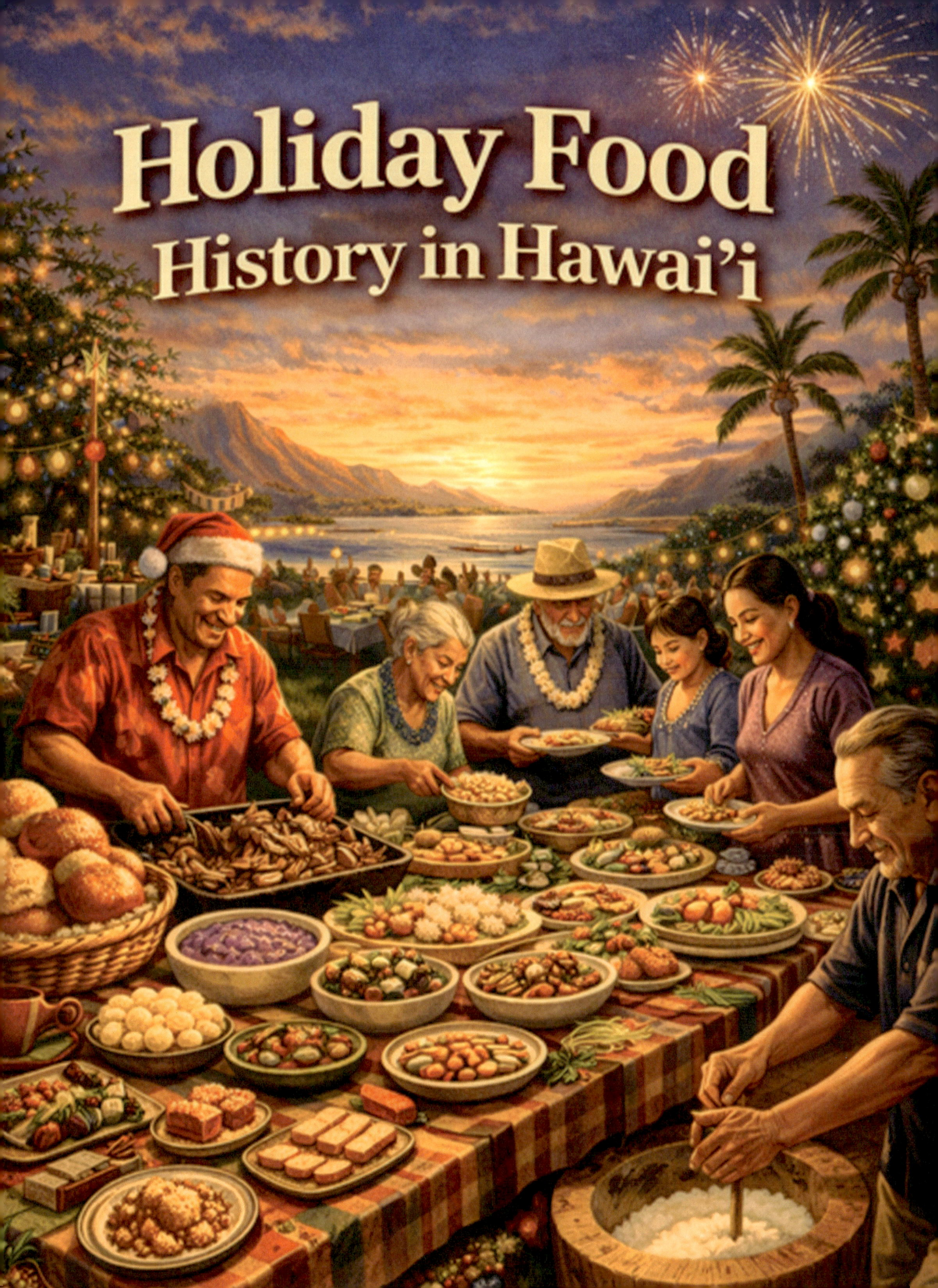

Holiday Food History in Hawai'i

Holiday food in Hawai'i tells the story of people, who arrived, who adapted, and who shared. Each major holiday reflects waves of migration, plantation life, and the enduring Hawaiian value of communal abundance. What appears on the table is never accidental; it is the result of history lived through food.

Rather than preserving a single "traditional" menu, Hawai'i's holiday meals continue to evolve, layer by layer, generation by generation.

Christmas: Abundance, Baking, and Plantation
Portuguese Influences: Sweet Bread & Malasadas

Portuguese laborers, primarily from Madeira and the Azores, brought with them rich baking traditions that became deeply woven into Christmas in Hawai'i. Sweet bread, soft, lightly sweet, enriched with eggs, became a holiday staple. It reflected both celebration and generosity, often baked in large loaves meant for sharing. Malasadas, though eaten year-round today, were closely tied to festive and religious occasions and became part of the broader holiday food memory.

These baked goods fit seamlessly into island life:
- Ingredients were accessible
- Recipes scaled easily for large families
- Sweetness symbolized celebration without excess

Over time, Portuguese breads became less "ethnic" and more simply local.

Plantation-Era Christmas Meals

During the plantation era, Christmas meals were shaped by necessity and diversity. Families cooked with what they had, often pooling resources with neighbors from different cultural backgrounds.

A plantation Christmas table might include:
- Rice as a central starch
- Slow-cooked meats meant to feed many
- Baked goods made in advance
- Desserts brought by different households

There was rarely a single "main dish." Instead, there was plenty, enough to share, enough to last, enough to give. Christmas became less about luxury and more about relief, rest, and togetherness after a long year of labor.

Christmas Timeline (Suggested Spread)
- Mid-1800s: Missionary-introduced Christmas observances
- Late 1800s–Early 1900s: Portuguese baking traditions take root
- Plantation Era: Potluck-style Christmas meals emerge
- Modern Day: Lū'au-style abundance replaces formal dining

Thanksgiving: Reinterpretation and Inclusion
Poi Instead of Mashed Potatoes

Thanksgiving entered Hawai'i as a mainland holiday, but it never remained unchanged. Local families adapted the meal to reflect island taste and availability. Poi often replaced mashed potatoes, not as a substitution, but as a natural choice. Its texture paired well with gravies, slow-cooked meats, and roasted turkey, while its cultural significance anchored the meal to place. Rice, too, became central, reflecting daily life in Hawai'i rather than seasonal novelty. These changes were not about rejection but belonging. Thanksgiving became a meal that made sense here.

Immigrant Influences on the Thanksgiving Table

Because Thanksgiving was adopted during a period of intense immigration, the holiday table became a reflection of Hawai'i's multicultural reality.

Depending on the household, dishes might include:
- Noodle dishes alongside stuffing
- Pickled vegetables instead of cranberry sauce
- Desserts reflecting Asian, European, or island influences

Thanksgiving in Hawai'i became less about recreating a mainland menu and more about expressing who was present at the table.

Thanksgiving Timeline (Suggested Spread)
- Late 1800s: Thanksgiving introduced through American influence
- Plantation Era: Local staples replace imported traditions
- Mid-1900s: Turkey remains, sides diversify
- Today: Thanksgiving becomes a fully local expression

New Year's: Renewal, Symbolism, and Intention
Japanese & Okinawan Influences

New Year's food traditions in Hawai'i are deeply influenced by Japanese and Okinawan communities, for whom the holiday carries strong spiritual and symbolic meaning.

Foods eaten at New Year are intentional:
- Mochi represents strength, continuity, and togetherness
- Soups resembling ozōni vary by household
- Prepared foods emphasize balance and renewal

These dishes are often made in advance, allowing New Year's Day itself to be a time of rest and reflection.

Symbolism of Food at New Year
New Year's meals emphasize meaning as much as flavor.

Common themes include:
- Long noodles for longevity
- Round foods for completeness and continuity
- Sweet flavors for hope and prosperity

In Hawai'i, these symbolic foods coexist with local staples, reflecting how cultural traditions remain distinct while still sharing the same table.

New Year's Timeline (Suggested Spread)
- Late 1800s: Japanese New Year traditions arrive in Hawai'i
- Early 1900s: Mochi-making becomes community-centered
- Mid-1900s: Traditions adapt to local ingredients
- Today: Symbolic foods continue alongside local dishes

NA Living History

Holiday food in Hawai'i is not frozen in time. It continues to change, shaped by new families, evolving tastes, and modern realities.

What remains constant is intention:
- Food prepared with care
- Dishes meant to be shared
- Tables that reflect who we are, not where traditions came from

This history lives on, not in museums, but in kitchens, garages, and backyard gatherings across the islands.

Ancestral & Modern Holiday Rituals
Rituals & Practices Beyond the Table

In Hawai'i, food is never separate from intention. Before a meal is prepared, before guests arrive, before hands are washed and plates are filled, there is awareness, of place, of people, and of what it means to gather. Holiday rituals, both ancestral and modern, are not rigid ceremonies. They are living practices that continue to evolve, shaped by 'ohana, faith, and personal history. Some are spoken aloud. Others are felt quietly. All are rooted in gratitude, connection, and respect.

Opening a Holiday Meal with Oli or Pule

Many families in Hawai'i begin holiday meals not with the first bite, but with words. For some, this takes the form of pule, a prayer reflecting Christian faith introduced through missionary influence and woven into generations of family practice. For others, an oli—a chant—may be offered to acknowledge ancestors, place, or the reason for gathering. Some families blend both. Others simply pause in silence. What matters is not the form, but the intention.

Opening a meal creates a moment of grounding:
- To acknowledge the labor that brought the food to the table
- To honor those who prepared it
- To remember those no longer physically present

This pause transforms a holiday meal from consumption into connection. Note for readers: If using oli or traditional chants, it is important to learn from appropriate sources and with permission.
Silence, spoken gratitude, or personal words are always valid expressions of respect.

Sharing Food with Neighbors & Kūpuna

One of the most enduring holiday practices in Hawai'i is giving food away. Plates are packed. Containers are filled. Extra portions are delivered to neighbors, elders, and those who may not be able to gather in large groups. This practice reflects the value of kōkua, helping without being asked, and reinforces that abundance is meant to circulate. For kūpuna especially, receiving food is more than nourishment. It is recognition, remembrance, and continuity.

Holiday cooking often includes an unspoken question:
> Who needs to be remembered today?
> Food becomes the answer.

New Year Cleansing Traditions
Physical & Spiritual Renewal

New Year in Hawai'i carries strong themes of clearing and renewal, influenced by both Hawaiian and Asian traditions. Cleansing may include:
- Cleaning the home before the new year arrives
- Letting go of broken or unused items
- Bathing or swimming as symbolic renewal
- Preparing food that represents fresh beginnings

These practices are not about perfection. They are about making space, physically, emotionally, and spiritually, for what comes next. Food prepared for the New Year often reflects this intention:
- Simple flavors
- Clear broths
- Foods made ahead to allow rest on the day itself

The act of preparation becomes part of the ritual.

Food Offerings & Gratitude Practices
In some households, a small portion of food is set aside, not to be eaten, but to be offered. This may be for:
- Ancestors
- Loved ones who have passed
- The ʻāina that provided the ingredients

Offerings can be formal or simple. A quiet moment. A whispered thank you. A plate left untouched. Gratitude practices remind us that food does not appear by chance. It comes from land, water, labor, and lineage. Holidays offer a natural time to acknowledge these relationships.

Living Rituals, Not Performances
It is important to understand that rituals in Hawaiʻi are not performances. They are not meant to be replicated perfectly or displayed. They are lived, adapted, and often deeply personal. Modern holiday rituals may look like:
- A moment of silence before eating
- Saying names of loved ones aloud
- Asking keiki to share what they're grateful for
- Choosing one dish to eat intentionally

These practices honor the past while allowing space for the present.

Reflection Prompts for the Holiday Table
You may wish to include these prompts at the beginning of a meal or while cooking:
- Who helped make this gathering possible?
- What does abundance look like for us this year?
- Who are we carrying with us today, in memory or in spirit?
- How can this meal extend beyond this table?

There are no right answers. The act of asking is enough.

Carrying Ritual Forward

Ancestral practices endure not because they are preserved unchanged, but because they are remembered with care.

Holiday rituals, whether spoken, shared, or quietly held, invite us to slow down, recognize our relationships, and gather with intention. They remind us that food is not only nourishment, but a vessel for memory, gratitude, and belonging.

The recipes that follow are offered in this spirit.

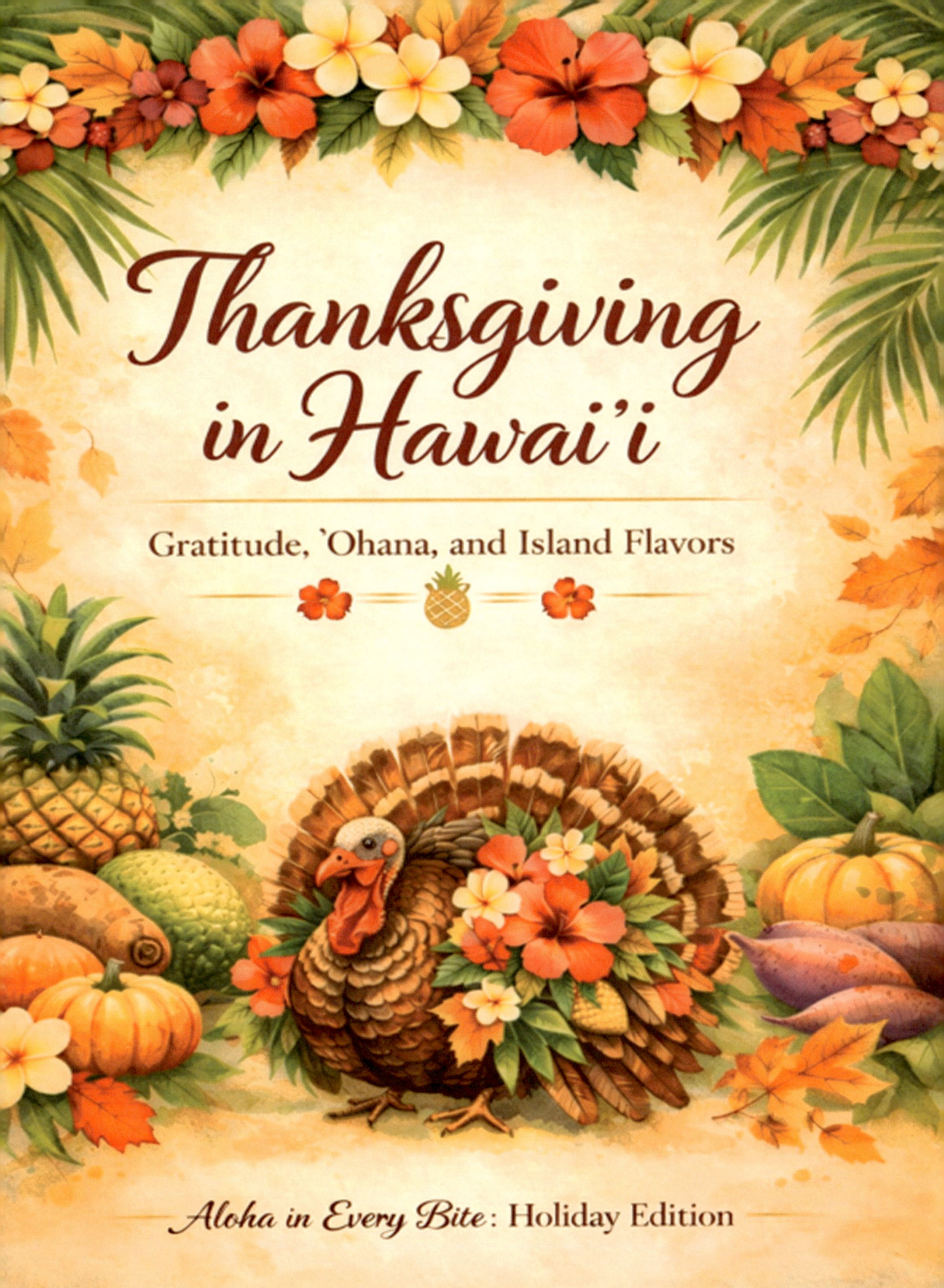

Cranberry Pineapple Compote with Hawaiian Ginger & Vanilla

CHEF'S NOTES

- Flavor Fusion: The tart cranberries and sweet pineapple balance perfectly, neither dominates, and the ginger adds gentle heat that makes it sparkle.
- Vanilla Layer: Adds depth and smoothness, rounding out acidity. For a stronger note, use a real vanilla bean.
- Texture Control: For a chunkier compote, cook less; for a smoother sauce, mash lightly with a fork once cooled.
- Make-Ahead: Best made 1–2 days in advance, flavors intensify overnight.

TASTING NOTES

- Aroma: Bright citrus and tropical fruit mingle with warm ginger and vanilla; sunshine meets holiday spice.
- Taste: Sweet-tart perfection, the cranberry's acidity softened by juicy pineapple and rounded by vanilla warmth.
- Texture: Glossy and luscious, with tender fruit pieces and a velvety syrup.
- Pairing Ideas:
    Serve with Kiawe-Smoked Turkey, Poi-Mashed Potatoes, or Macadamia-Coconut Rolls
    Use as a glaze base for Ham or Roasted Ulu (Breadfruit)
    Spoon over cheesecake or panna cotta for a holiday dessert twist

Cranberry Pineapple Compote with Hawaiian Ginger & Vanilla

A vibrant, chilled island salad fresh salmon, sweet onion, ripe tomato, and bursts of pomegranate for a festive twist

 COOK TIME: 20-25 MINS ★ ★ ★ DIFFICULTY: EASY  SERVINGS: 8-10

INGREDIENTS

- 12 oz (1 bag) fresh or frozen cranberries
- 1 cup finely chopped fresh pineapple (or crushed pineapple, drained)
- ¾ cup cane sugar or coconut sugar
- ¼ cup pineapple juice
- ¼ cup water
- 1–2 tsp freshly grated Hawaiian ginger (or standard ginger)
- 1 tsp vanilla extract or ½ vanilla bean, scraped
- Zest of 1 orange
- Juice of ½ orange
- Pinch of Hawaiian sea salt (pa'akai)
- Optional garnish: toasted coconut flakes or candied pineapple bits

INSTRUCTIONS

Simmer the Base

1. In a medium saucepan, combine sugar, water, pineapple juice, orange juice, and grated ginger.
2. Bring to a gentle simmer over medium heat, stirring until the sugar dissolves and the mixture becomes fragrant.

Add the Fruit

1. Stir in cranberries and orange zest.
2. Simmer 10–15 minutes, stirring occasionally, until the cranberries begin to burst and the mixture thickens slightly.
3. Add pineapple and continue cooking another 5–7 minutes until glossy and syrupy.

Finish and Cool

1. Remove from heat and stir in vanilla and a pinch of sea salt.
2. Allow to cool completely, it will thicken as it cools.
3. Store in a sealed container in the refrigerator for up to 7 days.

'Ilima & Macadamia Nut Bread Stuffing with Local Herbs

TASTING NOTES

- 'Ilima Blossoms: Traditionally symbolic of love and aloha, they add subtle floral aroma and bright color. Use sparingly, their flavor should whisper, not shout.
- Macadamia Nuts: Toast lightly before adding to enhance crunch and buttery depth.
- Make-Ahead Tip: Prepare up to the baking stage a day in advance; refrigerate, then bake before serving.
- Customization: Add diced Portuguese sausage (linguiça) or smoked tofu for a heartier version.

PAIRING IDEAS

- Aroma: Toasted bread, roasted nuts, and island herbs with a hint of floral sweetness.
- Taste: Rich and savory with gentle nuttiness, buttery texture, and bright herbal lift. The 'ilima provides a delicate, perfumed note that makes the dish feel festive and unique.
- Texture: Crispy on top, moist and tender inside, the perfect balance.
- Pairing Ideas:
    Serve with Kiawe-Smoked Turkey and Lilikoi Gravy
    Complements Cranberry-Pineapple Compote or Poi-Mashed Potatoes
    Try leftovers in a breakfast hash with eggs and a drizzle of chili oil

'Ilima & Macadamia Nut Bread Stuffing with Local Herbs

A Hawaiian twist on the classic stuffing, nutty, aromatic, and beautifully golden

 COOK TIME: 40-45 MINS   DIFFICULTY: MEDIUM   SERVINGS: 8-10

INGREDIENTS

For the Bread Base
- 1 loaf day-old sweet bread, Hawaiian rolls, or brioche, cubed (about 10 cups)
- ¾ cup toasted macadamia nuts, coarsely chopped
- 1 small Maui onion, finely diced
- 3 cloves garlic, minced
- 2 stalks celery, diced
- 1 small carrot, finely diced (optional)
- 2 Tbsp butter (or coconut oil for dairy-free)
- 1 Tbsp macadamia nut oil (optional for richness)

For the Liquid & Seasoning
- 2 cups chicken or vegetable stock
- 1 egg, lightly beaten (for binding)
- 1 tsp pa'akai (Hawaiian sea salt), or to taste
- ½ tsp cracked black pepper
- 1 Tbsp fresh thyme, chopped
- 1 Tbsp fresh sage, chopped
- 1 Tbsp fresh rosemary, chopped
- 2 Tbsp chopped 'ilima blossoms (or substitute edible flowers like nasturtium petals or marigold for color)
- 1 Tbsp chopped parsley or Chinese parsley (cilantro)
- ½ tsp chili pepper flakes (optional, for island heat)

INSTRUCTIONS

Prepare the Bread
1. Preheat oven to 350°F (175°C).
2. Spread bread cubes on a baking sheet and toast for 10–12 minutes until golden and lightly crisp.
3. Set aside to cool slightly.

Sauté the Aromatics
1. In a large skillet, melt butter and macadamia oil over medium heat.
2. Add onion, garlic, celery, and carrot.
3. Cook 5–7 minutes, stirring, until soft and fragrant.
4. Stir in herbs (thyme, sage, rosemary) and cook 1 more minute to bloom their flavors.

Combine & Season
1. In a large bowl, combine toasted bread cubes, sautéed vegetables, and macadamia nuts.
2. Add salt, pepper, and chili flakes if using.
3. In a separate bowl, whisk together stock and egg, then pour evenly over the mixture.
4. Add chopped 'ilima blossoms and parsley; gently toss until evenly moistened but not soggy.

Bake
1. Transfer to a greased 9x13-inch baking dish.
2. Cover with foil and bake for 25 minutes.
3. Uncover and bake another 15–20 minutes until the top is crisp and golden.

Charred Laua'o (or Kale) & Kou-Leaf Green Beans with Toasted Kukui Nuts

CHEF'S NOTES

- Laua'o Substitution: Laua'o (young taro leaves) are traditional and nutrient-rich but can be replaced with kale for accessibility. If using taro, always blanch thoroughly to remove calcium oxalate.
- Kukui Nuts: Known for their buttery texture and earthy depth, toast gently for 3–4 minutes max. If unavailable, macadamias make a great substitute.
- Island Smoke: Kiawe smoked salt enhances the greens charred edge, giving an imu (underground oven) essence.
- Make-Ahead Tip: Prepare nuts and blanch greens ahead; quickly char and combine before serving for perfect texture.

TASTING NOTES

- Aroma: Smoky greens with sweet onion and nutty richness, kissed by citrus.
- Taste: Savory, earthy, and lightly tangy, a balance of smoke, salt, and lime brightness.
- Texture: Crisp-tender beans, wilted greens, and crunchy toasted nuts.
- Pairing Ideas:
    Serve alongside Kiawe-Smoked Turkey or Hawaiian Ham with Paia Spice Glaze
    Pair with Poi-Mashed Potatoes or 'Ilima & Macadamia Bread Stuffing
    For a vegan holiday plate, combine with Lava-Rock Grilled Squash and Roasted 'Ulu Poke Relish

Charred Laua'o (or Kale) & Kou-Leaf Green Beans with Toasted Kukui Nuts

Earthy greens, smoky char, and buttery kukui crunch, a bold, modern take on Hawaiian greens for the holiday table

 COOK TIME: 15 MINS   ★ ★ ★ DIFFICULTY: EASY   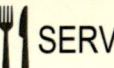 SERVINGS: 6

INGREDIENTS

For the Greens
- ½ lb. fresh green beans, ends trimmed
- 2 cups laua'o leaves (young taro greens) or kale (lacinato or baby kale)
- 1 Tbsp macadamia nut oil or olive oil
- 1 clove garlic, thinly sliced
- 1 small Maui onion, thinly sliced
- ½ tsp Kiawe smoked sea salt
- ¼ tsp freshly ground black pepper
- 1 Tbsp lime or calamansi juice

For the Kukui Nut Topping
- ¼ cup toasted kukui nuts (candlenuts), coarsely chopped
- 1 tsp soy sauce or tamari
- 1 tsp honey or coconut nectar
- Pinch of Hawaiian chili flakes (optional)
- Zest of ½ lime

Optional Garnish
- Microgreens or shredded dried seaweed (nori or ogo)
- Toasted sesame seeds

INSTRUCTIONS

Blanch and Shock the Green Beans
1. Bring a large pot of salted water to a boil.
2. Add green beans and cook 2 minutes until bright green and crisp-tender.
3. Transfer immediately to an ice bath to stop cooking. Drain and set aside.

Char the Greens
1. Heat a large cast-iron skillet or grill pan over medium-high heat.
2. Add oil, then scatter sliced onion and garlic. Cook until lightly caramelized.
3. Add kale or laua'o leaves (if using taro leaves, pre-blanch and drain to remove bitterness).
4. Toss with green beans and sear 2–3 minutes until edges char slightly.
5. Season with Kiawe smoked salt and pepper. Finish with lime juice for brightness.

Toast the Kukui Nuts
1. In a small skillet, toast chopped kukui nuts over medium heat until golden (3–4 minutes).
2. Add soy sauce, honey, chili flakes, and lime zest. Toss quickly until glossy and fragrant.
3. Remove from heat immediately, they burn fast!

Assemble
1. Arrange the charred greens and beans on a platter.
2. Sprinkle with warm kukui nut mixture.
3. Garnish with microgreens or a sprinkle of sesame seeds for color contrast.

Lava Rock Grilled Pumpkin or Butternut Squash Wedges with Coconut-Lime Butter

CHEF'S NOTES

- Lava-Rock Flavor: The porous stones hold and release heat evenly, giving the squash a deep, smoky note reminiscent of traditional imu-style cooking.
- Vegan Adaptation: Substitute coconut oil for butter, it enhances the tropical flavor beautifully.
- Citrus Trick: Add a splash of calamansi or Meyer lemon for extra dimension.
- Presentation Tip: Leave wedges slightly irregular, the rustic shape looks stunning on the table.

TASTING NOTES

- Aroma: Charred caramel, toasted coconut, and bright lime zest fill the air, smoky yet fresh.
- Taste: Sweet, buttery, and citrusy with undertones of smoke and spice. The coconut-lime butter ties it all together with creamy tang.
- Texture: Tender with crisp edges; each bite melts in the mouth with just enough chew from the grill.
- Pairing Ideas:
    Serve beside Kiawe-Smoked Turkey or Kalua Pork Roulade
    Pair with Coconut-Pineapple Crescent Rolls and Cranberry-Pineapple Compote for a complete flavor journey
    Top leftovers with a fried egg for a next-day tropical brunch

Lava Rock Grilled Pumpkin or Butternut Squash Wedges with Coconut-Lime Butter

Fire-kissed, caramelized squash with tropical creaminess and a burst of citrus

 COOK TIME: 25-30 MINS   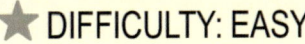 DIFFICULTY: EASY SERVINGS: 6-8

INGREDIENTS

For the Squash
- 1 medium pumpkin or large butternut squash (about 3–4 lbs.), peeled, seeded, and cut into 1-inch-thick wedges
- 2 Tbsp macadamia nut oil or olive oil
- 1 tsp Kiawe smoked sea salt (or smoked sea salt)
- ½ tsp freshly ground black pepper
- ½ tsp ground cinnamon
- ¼ tsp ground allspice
- 1 tsp brown sugar or coconut sugar (optional, for caramelization)

For the Coconut-Lime Butter
- 4 Tbsp unsalted butter (or coconut oil for vegan)
- 2 Tbsp coconut milk
- Zest and juice of 1 lime
- 1 tsp honey or agave syrup
- Pinch of Hawaiian sea salt (pa'akai)
- Optional: ½ tsp finely minced lemongrass for extra brightness

To Garnish
- Toasted coconut flakes
- Chopped fresh cilantro or mint
- Lime wedges

INSTRUCTIONS

Prepare the Squash
1. In a large bowl, toss squash wedges with oil, Kiawe smoked salt, pepper, cinnamon, allspice, and brown sugar.
2. Let sit 10–15 minutes while you prepare the grill.

Grill (Lava-Rock or Conventional Grill)
1. Heat a lava-rock grill (or charcoal/gas grill) to medium-high.
2. Lightly oil the grates.
3. Grill wedges for 4–5 minutes per side, turning until tender and caramelized with light charring.
4. Move to indirect heat or a cooler side of the grill to finish cooking if needed.

Make the Coconut-Lime Butter
1. In a small saucepan, melt butter over low heat.
2. Stir in coconut milk, lime zest, juice, honey, and salt.
3. Whisk gently until creamy and slightly emulsified.
4. Keep warm until serving.

Finish and Serve
1. Brush grilled squash with warm coconut-lime butter while still hot.
2. Arrange on a platter, drizzle any extra butter over the top.
3. Garnish with toasted coconut, herbs, and lime wedges.

Poi Mashed Potatoes (Taro-Infused Mash) with Roasted Garlic

CHEF'S NOTES

- Poi Balance: Use a medium consistency poi (not too thick or watery). Start with ¾ cup and adjust for desired flavor and texture.
- Cultural Harmony: Poi brings earthy taro flavor and soft purple hue, symbolizing connection to Hawaiian tradition.
- Flavor Layering: Roasted garlic adds depth and umami, balancing the subtle tang of poi.
- Vegan Option: Use coconut oil and coconut milk for a fully plant-based version that's still rich and aromatic.

TASTING NOTES

- Aroma: Gentle sweetness of roasted garlic, earthy taro undertones, and buttery warmth.
- Taste: Creamy and balanced, classic mashed potato comfort with the nutty, mineral depth of poi.
- Texture: Silky and velvety, with a faint chew from the taro's natural starch.
- Pairing Ideas:
    Serve alongside Kiawe-Smoked Turkey or Lilikoi Gravy
    Complements Kalua Pork, Sweet Potato Casserole, or Island Greens with Coconut-Lime Dressing

Poi Mashed Potatoes (Taro-Infused Mash) with Roasted Garlic

Creamy, earthy, and uniquely Hawaiian, a soulful side for any island feast

⏱ COOK TIME: 25 MINS ★ ★ ★ DIFFICULTY: EASY 🍴 SERVINGS: 6-8

INGREDIENTS

For the Mash
- 2 lbs. Yukon Gold or russet potatoes, peeled and cubed
- 1 cup poi (fresh or refrigerated, room temperature)
- 4 cloves roasted garlic (see below)
- 3 Tbsp butter (or coconut oil for dairy-free)
- ½ cup warm coconut milk or heavy cream
- ¼ cup chicken or vegetable stock (optional, for thinning)
- ½ tsp pa'akai (Hawaiian sea salt), or to taste
- ¼ tsp freshly ground black pepper
- 1 Tbsp chopped green onion (for garnish)

For the Roasted Garlic
- 1 whole garlic bulb
- 1 tsp olive or macadamia nut oil
- Pinch of sea salt

INSTRUCTIONS

Roast the Garlic
1. Preheat oven to 400°F (200°C).
2. Slice the top off the garlic bulb to expose cloves, drizzle with oil, and sprinkle with salt.
3. Wrap in foil and roast 30–35 minutes until soft, golden, and aromatic.
4. Cool slightly, then squeeze out the roasted garlic paste. Set aside.

Cook the Potatoes
1. Place potatoes in a pot of salted cold water.
2. Bring to a boil and cook until tender, about 15–20 minutes.
3. Drain and return to the pot to evaporate excess moisture.

Mash and Infuse
1. Add butter, roasted garlic, and coconut milk to the hot potatoes.
2. Mash until smooth and creamy.
3. Fold in the poi gently, don't overmix or it can become sticky.
4. Adjust consistency with a splash of warm stock if needed.
5. Season with pa'akai and black pepper to taste.

Serve
Transfer to a serving bowl, top with a pat of butter and sprinkle with chopped green onion. Serve warm.

Spiced Sweet Potato Casserole with Macadamia Nut & Coconut-Pineapple Crust

CHEF'S NOTES

- Island Upgrade: The pineapple adds brightness and acidity that balance the sweetness, while macadamia nuts bring a rich, buttery crunch.
- Make-Ahead: You can prepare the sweet potato layer a day ahead and refrigerate. Add the crust and bake before serving.
- Texture Tip: For extra crunch, toast the macadamia nuts and coconut beforehand.
- Flavor Harmony: The touch of orange zest and cinnamon ties the tropical and traditional holiday flavors together.

TASTING NOTES

- Aroma: Like a Hawaiian holiday, warm spices, roasted nuts, toasted coconut, and caramelized pineapple waft through the air.
- Taste: Silky sweet potato meets buttery macadamia, kissed by tropical fruit. Each bite balances earthy depth and island brightness.
- Texture: Creamy base, crisp golden crust, indulgent yet light.
- Pairing Ideas: Serve alongside Kiawe-Smoked Turkey or Kalua Pork Roulade for a perfect balance of savory and sweet.

Spiced Sweet Potato Casserole with Macadamia Nut & Coconut-Pineapple Crust

A tropical twist on a Thanksgiving and Christmas classic

COOK TIME: 40-45 MINS ★ ★ ☆ DIFFICULTY: MEDIUM SERVINGS: 8-10

INGREDIENTS

For the Sweet Potato Base
- 3 lbs. sweet potatoes ('uala), peeled and cubed
- ¼ cup unsalted butter (or coconut oil for dairy-free)
- ¼ cup coconut milk (or heavy cream for richness)
- ¼ cup brown sugar or coconut sugar
- 2 Tbsp honey or maple syrup
- 1 tsp ground cinnamon
- ½ tsp ground nutmeg
- ½ tsp ground ginger
- ½ tsp Hawaiian sea salt (pa'akai)
- 1 tsp vanilla extract
- Zest of 1 orange
- 2 eggs, lightly beaten

For the Coconut-Pineapple Macadamia Crust
- ¾ cup crushed pineapple, drained
- ¾ cup shredded coconut (unsweetened preferred)
- ¾ cup chopped roasted macadamia nuts
- ½ cup brown sugar
- ¼ cup flour (or tapioca flour for gluten-free)
- 3 Tbsp melted butter (or coconut oil)
- Pinch of sea salt

INSTRUCTIONS

Cook and Mash the Sweet Potatoes
1. Bring a large pot of salted water to a boil. Add sweet potatoes and cook until tender, about 15–20 minutes.
2. Drain and mash until smooth.

Mix the Base
1. Stir in butter, coconut milk, sugar, honey, spices, salt, vanilla, and orange zest while the potatoes are still warm.
2. Whisk in beaten eggs until well combined and silky.
3. Spread mixture evenly in a buttered 9x13-inch baking dish.

Prepare the Crust
1. In a medium bowl, combine pineapple, shredded coconut, macadamia nuts, brown sugar, flour, and melted butter.
2. Mix until crumbly and evenly coated.

Assemble and Bake
1. Sprinkle the crust mixture evenly over the sweet potato layer.
2. Bake at 350°F (175°C) for 35–40 minutes, until the topping is golden and bubbly.
3. Cool for 10 minutes before serving, it will firm slightly as it sets.

Hawaiian Style Turkey with Kiawe Smoked Sea Salt & Pa'akai Rub

CHEF'S NOTES

- Flavor Layering: The Kiawe smoked salt provides a gentle island smokiness without needing a smoker. The pa'akai deepens minerality and umami, the true flavor of the sea.
- Macadamia Nut Oil: Adds buttery richness and helps the rub caramelize beautifully.
- Island Touch: The pineapple juice in the roasting pan creates an aromatic steam that keeps the bird moist and infuses a subtle tropical sweetness.
- Make It Grilled: For an authentic Hawaiian feel, try finishing the turkey over a kiawe wood grill for 10–15 minutes after roasting.

TASTING NOTES

- Aroma: Smoky-sweet with warm citrus and hints of island herbs.
- Taste: Deeply savory and earthy with balanced salt and caramelized edges. The citrus zest brightens the richness, while the smoke and sea-minerality tie it to the islands.
- Texture: Juicy, tender meat under crisp golden skin, a perfect contrast of crunch and succulence.
- Pairing Ideas: Serve with poi-mashed potatoes, coconut-lime green beans, and cranberry-pineapple compote for a full Hawaiian Thanksgiving spread.

Hawaiian Style Turkey with Kiawe Smoked Sea Salt & Pa'akai Rub

A centerpiece that celebrates island flavor, smoke, and spirit

COOK TIME: 3.5-4 HOURS — **DIFFICULTY: MEDIUM** — **SERVINGS: 8-10**

INGREDIENTS

For the Turkey
- 1 whole turkey (12–14 lbs.), thawed
- 2 Tbsp Kiawe smoked sea salt (or substitute smoked Hawaiian sea salt)
- 1 Tbsp pa'akai (Hawaiian pink sea salt)
- 1 ½ Tbsp brown sugar or coconut sugar
- 2 tsp fresh cracked black pepper
- 1 tsp ground allspice
- 1 tsp Hawaiian chili pepper flakes (or substitute red pepper flakes)
- 1 tsp garlic powder
- 1 tsp onion powder
- Zest of 1 orange and 1 lime
- 3 Tbsp macadamia nut oil (or light olive oil)
- 3 sprigs fresh rosemary
- 3 sprigs fresh thyme
- 1 bunch fresh sage
- 1 cup pineapple juice
- ½ cup chicken or turkey stock

Optional Hawaiian Brine (for deeper flavor)
- 1 gallon water
- ½ cup pa'akai or sea salt
- ½ cup brown sugar
- 4 cloves garlic, smashed
- 1 inch piece fresh ginger, sliced
- 1 orange, sliced
- 2 bay leaves
- 1 Tbsp whole peppercorns
- ½ cup pineapple juice

INSTRUCTIONS

Brine the Turkey (optional but recommended)
1. In a large stockpot, bring all brine ingredients to a gentle simmer until sugar and salt dissolve.
2. Cool completely, then submerge turkey (add ice if needed).
3. Refrigerate 12–24 hours. Remove, pat completely dry.

Prepare the Rub
1. In a small bowl, combine Kiawe smoked sea salt, pa'akai, brown sugar, pepper, allspice, chili flakes, garlic and onion powder, and citrus zest.
2. Mix in macadamia nut oil to create a coarse paste.

Season and Rest
1. Rub the mixture generously over the turkey, including under the skin where possible.
2. Place herbs (rosemary, thyme, sage) inside the cavity.
3. Let rest uncovered in the fridge for 2–3 hours (or overnight) to allow the rub to penetrate and the skin to dry slightly for crispness.

Roast
1. Preheat oven to 325°F (165°C).
2. Place turkey breast-side up on a rack in a roasting pan. Add pineapple juice and stock to the bottom for steam and aromatics.
3. Roast uncovered 3½–4 hours, basting every 30 minutes with the pan juices.
4. Tent loosely with foil if the skin browns too quickly.
5. Internal temperature should reach 165°F (74°C) at the thickest part of the thigh.

Rest and Carve
1. Transfer turkey to a cutting board, tent with foil, and rest 20–30 minutes before carving.
2. Use pan drippings to make a Lilikoi-Pineapple Gravy (optional pairing).

Lilikoi (Passion Fruit) Gravy with Drippings & Island Herbs

CHEF'S NOTES

- Flavor Harmony: The lilikoi delivers acidity that brightens roasted meats, while pineapple softens it with tropical sweetness.
- Kiawe Smoked Salt: Adds subtle depth and pairs beautifully with turkey or pork.
- Make-Ahead Tip: This gravy can be made up to 2 days ahead and reheated gently before serving, whisk to restore smoothness.
- Vegetarian Option: Skip drippings and use mushroom stock plus macadamia oil for a rich plant-based version.

TASTING NOTES

- Aroma: Fresh herbs, island fruit, and a whisper of smoke, like a luau meets Sunday roast.
- Taste: Tart passion fruit balances savory roasted flavors; herbs add depth and aroma while cream ties everything together.
- Texture: Silky, rich, and pourable, coats turkey perfectly without heaviness.
- Pairing Ideas:
    Over Kiawe-Smoked Turkey or Kalua Pork Roulade
    Drizzled on Poi-Mashed Potatoes
    As a glaze base for Ulu (Breadfruit) Wedges

Lilikoi (Passion Fruit) Gravy with Drippings & Island Herbs

A bright, tropical take on classic gravy, silky, savory, and kissed with island sunshine

COOK TIME: 15-20 MINS ★ ★ ★ DIFFICULTY: EASY SERVINGS: 2 CUPS

INGREDIENTS

- 3 Tbsp pan drippings from roast turkey or poultry
- 2 Tbsp butter (or macadamia nut oil for a nutty island flavor)
- 3 Tbsp flour (or tapioca flour for gluten-free)
- ½ cup lilikoi (passion fruit) puree or juice
- ½ cup pineapple juice
- 1 cup unsalted turkey or chicken stock (or vegetable stock)
- ½ tsp Kiawe smoked sea salt
- ¼ tsp pa'akai (Hawaiian sea salt)
- ¼ tsp cracked black pepper
- 1 tsp finely chopped fresh thyme
- 1 tsp fresh sage, minced
- ½ tsp rosemary, minced
- ½ tsp honey or coconut sugar (optional, to balance acidity)
- 2 Tbsp heavy cream or coconut cream (optional for richness)

INSTRUCTIONS

Start the Base
1. In a saucepan over medium heat, melt the butter and pan drippings together.
2. Whisk in flour to create a roux. Cook 1–2 minutes until lightly golden and nutty, this builds body and depth.

Add the Island Flavors
1. Slowly pour in the lilikoi and pineapple juices, whisking to smooth out lumps.
2. Simmer for 2–3 minutes, allowing the tropical acidity to mellow.

Build and Balance
1. Gradually whisk in the stock. Bring to a gentle simmer and cook 8–10 minutes, whisking occasionally, until thickened and glossy.
2. Stir in Kiawe smoked salt, pa'akai, pepper, and fresh herbs.
3. Taste, adjust salt and add honey if the lilikoi is particularly tart.

Finish
Whisk in cream or coconut cream for a velvety finish. For a smooth presentation, strain through a fine mesh sieve before serving warm.

Mango-Papaya Pie with Macadamia Crust and Coconut-Whipped Cream

CHEF'S NOTES

- Coconut Milk Tip: Use only full-fat coconut milk and chill it well so the cream separates cleanly.
- Flavor Balance: The lime and sea salt brighten the fruit, preventing the dessert from being overly sweet.
- Make-Ahead: The crust and filling can be made a day ahead. Assemble and top before serving for best texture.
- Variation: Add a drizzle of passion fruit (lilikoi) syrup for extra tartness and color contrast.

TASTING NOTES

- Aroma: Tropical fruit perfume with buttery macadamia richness and hints of vanilla.
- Taste: Layers of tangy mango, mellow papaya, and nutty crust, lifted by cool, airy coconut cream.
- Texture: Creamy filling meets crumbly, buttery crunch; the coconut whip melts into each bite.
- Pairing Ideas:
    Serve after Kiawe-Smoked Turkey or Kalua Pork Roulade for a bright finish
    Pair with a Lilikoi Spritz or Sparkling Guava Cooler
    Garnish with edible flowers like 'ilima or orchids for a show-stopping presentation

 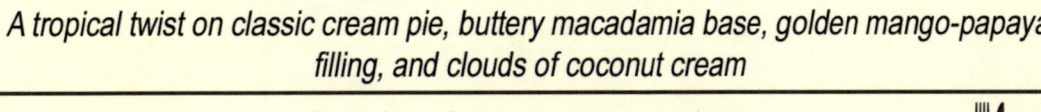

Mango-Papaya Pie with Macadamia Crust and Coconut-Whipped Cream

A tropical twist on classic cream pie, buttery macadamia base, golden mango-papaya filling, and clouds of coconut cream

 COOK TIME: 20 MINS   DIFFICULTY: MEDIUM SERVINGS: 8

INGREDIENTS

For the Macadamia Crust
- 1½ cups crushed macadamia nuts (lightly toasted)
- 1 cup graham cracker crumbs or crushed vanilla wafers
- ¼ cup brown sugar
- 5 Tbsp melted butter (or coconut oil for dairy-free)
- Pinch of Hawaiian sea salt (pa'akai)

For the Mango-Papaya Filling
- 2 cups fresh ripe mango (about 2 large), peeled and diced
- 1½ cups ripe papaya (about 1 medium), peeled and diced
- ¼ cup sugar or coconut sugar (adjust based on fruit sweetness)
- 1 Tbsp fresh lime juice
- 2 tsp cornstarch mixed with 1 Tbsp water (for thickening)
- 1 tsp vanilla extract
- ¼ tsp ground cardamom or allspice (optional for warmth)
- Pinch of pa'akai

For the Coconut-Whipped Cream
- 1 (13.5 oz) can full-fat coconut milk, chilled overnight
- 2 Tbsp powdered sugar or honey
- ½ tsp vanilla extract
- Optional: zest of 1 lime

INSTRUCTIONS

Prepare the Crust
1. Preheat oven to 350°F (175°C).
2. In a bowl, combine macadamia nuts, crumbs, sugar, butter, and salt.
3. Press mixture firmly into a 9-inch pie pan, covering bottom and sides evenly.
4. Bake 10–12 minutes until lightly golden and fragrant.
5. Cool completely before adding filling.

Cook the Filling
1. In a saucepan over medium heat, combine mango, papaya, sugar, lime juice, vanilla, cardamom, and a pinch of salt.
2. Cook 8–10 minutes, stirring often, until fruit softens and releases juices.
3. Stir in cornstarch slurry and cook 1–2 minutes until thick and glossy.
4. Remove from heat, taste for sweetness, and cool slightly.

Assemble the Pie
1. Spoon the cooled fruit filling into the crust, spreading evenly.
2. Chill in the refrigerator for at least 2 hours to set.

Make the Coconut-Whipped Cream
1. Scoop the solid coconut cream from the top of the chilled can into a mixing bowl.
2. Add powdered sugar and vanilla.
3. Beat with an electric mixer on medium-high until fluffy and smooth (about 2–3 minutes).
4. Fold in lime zest for brightness, if desired.

Serve
Top chilled pie with generous clouds of coconut whipped cream and a sprinkle of toasted macadamia nuts or fresh mango slices.

Kona Coffee & Kiawe Smoked Sea Salt Caramel Pecan Bars

CHEF'S NOTES

- Kona Coffee Depth: Brew it strong, the bittersweet note balances caramel richness and adds sophistication.
- Kiawe Smoked Salt Magic: Adds a whisper of island smoke, echoing the flavor of roasted pecans and caramelized sugar.
- Nut Variation: Use a half-and-half mix of pecans and macadamias for texture contrast and buttery flavor.
- Texture Control: For chewier bars, reduce baking time slightly; for crisper edges, extend 3–5 minutes.
- Make-Ahead: Keeps up to 5 days in an airtight container, flavor deepens over time.

TASTING NOTES

- Aroma: Buttery caramel, roasted nuts, and rich coffee with a smoky finish, like a warm Hawaiian café at sunset.
- Taste: Sweet, nutty, and toffee-like with earthy coffee tones; the sea salt heightens every bite.
- Texture: Crisp shortbread base, gooey caramel center, and crunchy toasted nuts, satisfying layers of contrast.
- Pairing Ideas:
    Serve with Hawaiian Vanilla Ice Cream or Coconut Gelato
    Enjoy alongside Kona Espresso or a Dark Rum Old Fashioned
    Wrap individually for holiday gift boxes, they travel beautifully

Kona Coffee & Kiawe Smoked Sea Salt Caramel Pecan Bars

A decadent island treat, buttery shortbread, Kona-infused caramel, toasted pecans, and a kiss of smoked sea salt

 COOK TIME: 35-40 MINS   DIFFICULTY: MEDIUM   SERVINGS: 16 BARS

INGREDIENTS

For the Shortbread Base
- 1 cup (2 sticks) unsalted butter, softened
- ½ cup brown sugar
- 2 cups all-purpose flour
- ¼ tsp pa'akai (Hawaiian sea salt)
- 1 tsp vanilla extract

For the Kona Coffee Caramel Layer
- 1 cup granulated sugar
- ½ cup brown sugar
- ½ cup heavy cream
- ¼ cup Kona coffee (strongly brewed)
- ½ cup unsalted butter
- ½ tsp Kiawe smoked sea salt (plus extra for garnish)
- 1½ cups toasted pecan halves (or substitute macadamia nuts or mix both!)
- 1 tsp vanilla extract

INSTRUCTIONS

Prepare the Shortbread
1. Preheat oven to 350°F (175°C).
2. Line a 9x13-inch baking pan with parchment paper, leaving an overhang for easy removal.
3. In a bowl, cream butter and brown sugar until fluffy.
4. Add flour, sea salt, and vanilla; mix until a crumbly dough forms.
5. Press evenly into the prepared pan.
6. Bake 15–18 minutes until lightly golden. Cool slightly.

Make the Kona Coffee Caramel
1. In a medium saucepan, combine sugars, butter, cream, and Kona coffee over medium heat.
2. Stir constantly until the mixture comes to a gentle boil.
3. Reduce heat slightly and simmer 4–6 minutes, stirring often, until thickened and glossy.
4. Remove from heat; stir in vanilla, Kiawe smoked salt, and toasted pecans.
5. Immediately pour caramel mixture over the shortbread base, spreading evenly.

Bake Again
1. Return to the oven and bake for 12–15 minutes until bubbling and golden-brown on top.
2. Sprinkle lightly with additional Kiawe smoked sea salt while hot.
3. Cool completely before cutting into bars.

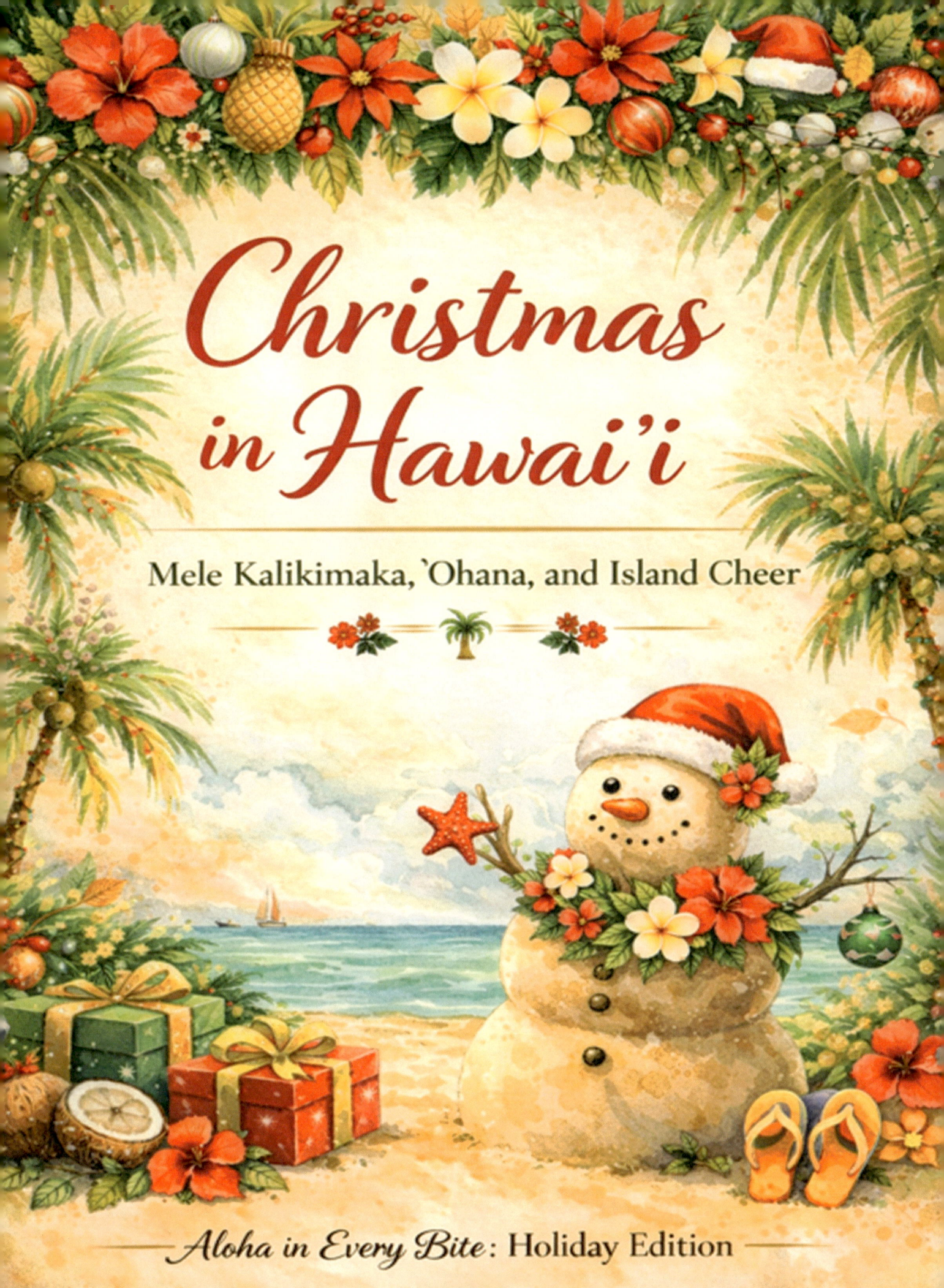

Hibiscus Cranberry Mocktail with Sparkling Guava

TASTING NOTES

- Aroma: Floral and fruity with hints of citrus and tropical guava.
- Taste: Bright and refreshing cranberry tang balanced by smooth guava sweetness and hibiscus depth.
- Texture: Lightly effervescent with crisp acidity and juicy pomegranate bursts.
- Color: Deep ruby-red with soft pink foam as festive as a Maui sunset.

PAIRING IDEAS

- Perfect pre-dinner toast alongside Cranberry–Pineapple Compote or Poi-Mashed Potatoes
- Serve with desserts like Molasses–Gingerbread Haupia Cupcakes or Candied Macadamias
- Beautiful in a carafe or punch bowl for a tropical Christmas or New Year's celebration

Hibiscus Cranberry Mocktail with Sparkling Guava

A vibrant island mocktail tart hibiscus tea meets cranberry and guava sparkle for a naturally festive Hawaiian toast

 COOK TIME: 10 MINS   DIFFICULTY: EASY   SERVINGS: 4

INGREDIENTS

For the Hibiscus Base
- 2 cups brewed hibiscus tea (from dried hibiscus flowers or tea bags), cooled
- 1 cup 100% cranberry juice (unsweetened preferred)
- 2 Tbsp lime juice
- 3–4 Tbsp honey, agave, or simple syrup (adjust to taste)
- Pinch of Pa'akai (Hawaiian sea salt) to enhance flavor

To Finish
- 1½ cups sparkling guava soda or sparkling water with guava nectar
- Crushed ice or large ice cubes
- Optional: ¼ cup pomegranate arils or thin guava slices for garnish

Garnish
- Lime wheels or dehydrated citrus
- Edible hibiscus petals or orchids
- Sprig of fresh mint

INSTRUCTIONS

Brew the Base
1. Steep hibiscus flowers or tea bags in 2½ cups hot water for 5–6 minutes.
2. Strain and let cool completely.
3. In a pitcher, combine hibiscus tea, cranberry juice, lime juice, honey (to taste), and a small pinch of salt. Stir well.
4. Chill for at least 15 minutes before serving.

Assemble the Mocktail
1. Fill glasses halfway with ice.
2. Pour the hibiscus–cranberry mix halfway up each glass.
3. Top with sparkling guava soda to fill.
4. Gently stir once to blend the layers the deep red base and pink bubbles will create a sunset ombré effect.

Garnish & Serve
- Add pomegranate arils for sparkle and texture.
- Garnish each glass with a lime wheel, mint sprig, and an edible flower.
- Serve chilled, immediately after topping with bubbles for maximum effervescence.

Lomi Lomi Salmon Salad with Pomegranate & Maui Onion

CHEF'S NOTES

- Lomi Lomi Tradition: This dish traditionally uses salted salmon "massaged" with tomato and onion here, the pomegranate adds sparkle and holiday sweetness.
- Pomegranate Pop: Adds a beautiful red hue and juicy contrast, symbolizing festivity and abundance.
- Make-Ahead Tip: Cure salmon a day in advance; mix salad ingredients right before serving for freshness.
- Island Upgrade: For a twist, top with diced avocado or drizzle of coconut-lime dressing.

TASTING NOTES

- Aroma: Fresh ocean breeze, citrus, and sweet Maui onion crisp and clean.
- Taste: Balanced and refreshing salty, tangy, sweet, and slightly spicy. The pomegranate bursts cut through the richness of the salmon.
- Texture: Silky fish, crisp onion, juicy fruit, and a hint of crunch from pomegranate.
- Pairing Ideas:
  - Serve as a chilled side for Kiawe-Smoked Turkey or Kalua Pork Roulade
  - Pair with Coconut–Pineapple Crescent Rolls and a Lilikoi Spritz
  - Makes an elegant starter for any island-style Christmas or New Year's dinner

Lomi Lomi Salmon Salad with Pomegranate & Maui Onion

A vibrant, chilled island salad fresh salmon, sweet onion, ripe tomato, and bursts of pomegranate for a festive twist

 COOK TIME: 25 MINS   DIFFICULTY: EASY SERVINGS: 6-8

INGREDIENTS

For the Salmon
- 1 lb fresh salmon fillet (skinless, sushi-grade preferred)
- 2 Tbsp Hawaiian Sea salt (Pa'akai)
- ½ tsp sugar
- 1 tsp lime or lemon zest

For the Salad
- 2 large ripe tomatoes, diced small
- ½ medium Maui onion, finely diced
- ½ cup pomegranate arils (fresh, not syrup)
- 1 small green onion, sliced thin
- 1 Tbsp chopped fresh cilantro or parsley
- 1 tsp finely chopped Hawaiian chili (optional, for heat)
- 1 Tbsp fresh lime juice
- 1 Tbsp olive oil or macadamia nut oil
- ½ tsp Kiawe smoked sea salt (or more to taste)
- Cracked black pepper to taste

For Garnish
- Extra pomegranate arils
- Edible flowers or microgreens
- Lime wedges

INSTRUCTIONS

Cure the Salmon
1. Rinse salmon and pat dry.
2. Mix sea salt, sugar, and zest; rub evenly over salmon on both sides.
3. Wrap tightly in plastic wrap and refrigerate for 2–3 hours (or up to overnight for deeper flavor).
4. Rinse off the cure under cold water, pat dry again, and dice into ¼-inch cubes. Chill until ready to mix.

Build the Salad
1. In a chilled bowl, combine diced salmon, tomatoes, Maui onion, pomegranate, green onion, and herbs.
2. Add lime juice, oil, and chili (if using).
3. Toss gently to coat the "lomi lomi" (to massage) technique gives the salad its name.
4. Adjust seasoning with Kiawe salt and pepper.
5. Chill for at least 30 minutes before serving to let flavors marry.

Serve
Spoon into a chilled serving bowl or platter. Garnish with extra pomegranate, herbs, or edible flowers for color and texture contrast. Serve cold.

Candied Mauna Loa Macadamias in Dark Chocolate & Sea Salt

CHEF'S NOTES

- Caramelization Tip: Don't walk away during the candying stage sugar goes from perfect to burnt quickly. The goal is a light amber caramel, not dark brown.
- Salt Balance: The pa'akai highlights sweetness and the chocolate's depth never skip the finishing sprinkle.
- Chocolate Quality: Choose a dark chocolate with fruity notes (like Hawaiian-origin cacao or 70%
- bittersweet). It harmonizes beautifully with the buttery nuts.
- Make It Luxe: Drizzle with white chocolate or dust lightly with edible gold for holiday flair.

TASTING NOTES

- Aroma: Buttery caramel and roasted macadamia with rich cocoa and a hint of sea air.
- Taste: A dance of sweet, salty, and bitter roasted macadamia crunch, smooth dark chocolate, and subtle smoky salt.
- Texture: Snappy chocolate shell, crunchy caramel center, buttery melt.
- Pairing Ideas:
  - Serve with Kona Coffee, Lilikoi Mimosas, or Rum-Spiced Eggnog
  - Use as garnish over Mango-Papaya Pie or Haupia Cupcakes
  - Perfect as edible gifts or as part of a Holiday Charcuterie of Sweets

Candied Mauna Loa Macadamias in Dark Chocolate & Sea Salt

Golden caramelized macadamias dipped in silky dark chocolate and dusted with Hawaiian sea salt the ultimate island confection

 COOK TIME: 35 MINS   DIFFICULTY: EASY   SERVINGS: 20

INGREDIENTS

- 2 cups whole Mauna Loa macadamia nuts (raw or lightly roasted)
- ½ cup granulated sugar
- 2 Tbsp water
- 1 Tbsp unsalted butter
- ½ tsp pa'akai (Hawaiian sea salt), plus extra for garnish
- 8 oz high-quality dark chocolate (60–70% cacao), chopped or chips
- 1 tsp coconut oil (for glossy coating)
- Optional: pinch of Kiawe smoked salt for finishing
- Optional garnish: gold dust, edible flowers, or toasted coconut shavings

INSTRUCTIONS

Candy the Macadamias
1. Line a baking sheet with parchment paper.
2. In a heavy saucepan over medium heat, combine sugar and water. Stir until sugar dissolves and starts to bubble.
3. Add macadamia nuts and stir constantly as the syrup thickens and begins to crystallize around the nuts.
4. Keep stirring until sugar remelts into a golden caramel that evenly coats the nuts (8–10 minutes total).
5. Quickly stir in butter and a pinch of pa'akai, then spread nuts onto the prepared sheet to cool completely. Break apart once hardened.

Melt the Chocolate
1. Place chocolate and coconut oil in a heatproof bowl.
2. Melt gently over a double boiler (or microwave in 20-second intervals), stirring until smooth and glossy.

Dip and Finish
1. Using a fork or dipping tool, coat each candied macadamia in melted chocolate, letting excess drip off.
2. Place on parchment paper and sprinkle immediately with sea salt (or Kiawe smoked salt for a deeper finish).
3. Let set at room temperature for 20–30 minutes, or refrigerate for 10–15 minutes to speed up.

Store or Gift
Once fully set, store in an airtight container at cool room temperature for up to 2 weeks or package in small glass jars or gift tins tied with raffia and dried flowers for a beautiful island-inspired holiday gift.

Coconut Pineapple Crescent Rolls

CHEF'S NOTES
- Island Touch: The crushed pineapple adds gentle sweetness and tenderness, don't skip it!
- Dairy-Free Option: Substitute coconut oil and coconut milk throughout; the rolls become even more aromatic.
- Make-Ahead Tip: Shape and refrigerate rolls overnight; bake fresh in the morning for brunch.
- Serving Style: These shine at dinner but also make a dreamy breakfast roll with passion fruit butter or guava jam.

TASTING NOTES
- Aroma: Freshly baked bread with buttery coconut notes and a whisper of pineapple.
- Taste: Subtle sweetness layered with richness, not dessert-sweet, but perfectly tropical and comforting.
- Texture: Soft and pillowy inside, lightly crisp on the outside from the glaze.
- Pairing Ideas:
    Serve warm with Lilikoi (Passion Fruit) Butter or Macadamia Honey
    Perfect alongside Kiawe-Smoked Turkey or Kalua Pork Roulade
    For brunch, pair with Kona Coffee or a Pineapple Mimosa

Coconut Pineapple Crescent Rolls

Buttery, fluffy dinner rolls with tropical flair golden, crescents brushed with coconut glaze and a hint of pineapple sunshine

 COOK TIME: 15-18 MINS   DIFFICULTY: MEDIUM   SERVINGS: 12

INGREDIENTS

For the Dough
- 3¼ cups all-purpose flour (plus extra for kneading)
- ¼ cup sugar
- 1 packet (2¼ tsp) instant yeast
- ½ tsp pa'akai (Hawaiian sea salt)
- ½ cup warm coconut milk (100–110°F)
- ¼ cup crushed pineapple (drained, but reserve juice)
- ¼ cup pineapple juice (from drained fruit)
- ¼ cup unsalted butter, melted (or coconut oil for dairy-free)
- 1 large egg
- 1 tsp vanilla extract

For Brushing & Finishing
- 2 Tbsp melted butter (or coconut oil)
- 2 Tbsp coconut milk
- 1 Tbsp honey or simple syrup
- Optional garnish: shredded coconut or coarse sea salt

INSTRUCTIONS

Activate and Mix
1. In a large mixing bowl, combine warm coconut milk, pineapple juice, sugar, and yeast. Let sit for 5 minutes, until foamy.
2. Stir in melted butter, egg, vanilla, and crushed pineapple.
3. Add flour and salt gradually, mixing until a soft dough forms.

Knead and Rise
1. Transfer dough to a lightly floured surface and knead for 8–10 minutes until smooth and elastic.
2. Place in a greased bowl, cover with a damp towel, and let rise in a warm place for 1 hour or until doubled in size.

Shape the Crescents
1. Punch down dough and roll into a 12-inch circle about ¼ inch thick.
2. Cut into 12 even wedges (like pizza slices).
3. Starting from the wide end, roll each wedge into a crescent shape.
4. Place on a parchment-lined baking sheet, point side down. Cover and let rise another 30 minutes.

Bake
1. Preheat oven to 375°F (190°C).
2. Bake 15–18 minutes until golden brown and lightly fragrant.
3. While still warm, brush with glaze mixture (see below).

Coconut-Pineapple Glaze
Whisk together melted butter, coconut milk, and honey until smooth. Brush generously over warm rolls for shine and tropical aroma. Sprinkle with shredded coconut or a pinch of pa'akai if desired.

Roasted 'Ulu (Breadfruit) with Poke-Style Relish: Ahi, Limu & Local Chili

CHEF'S NOTES

- Texture Tip: Roast 'ulu until crisp on the outside and tender inside it should mimic roasted potatoes but with a nutty, bread-like body.
- Fish Quality: Always use sashimi-grade ahi the dish shines on freshness. For a vegan version, substitute diced hearts of palm or tofu.
- Limu: If limu kohu is unavailable, use ogo or wakame for briny ocean flavor.
- Serving Style: Works beautifully as a shared platter or elegant small plate starter.

TASTING NOTES

- Aroma: Smoky roasted 'ulu, sesame oil, and the sea-breeze scent of limu.
- Taste: The 'ulu's subtle sweetness contrasts perfectly with salty, spicy ahi a harmony of land and ocean.
- Texture: Creamy breadfruit base topped with tender poke and crunchy sesame silky, juicy, and crisp in each bite.
- Pairing Ideas:
    - Serve as an appetizer before Kalua Pork Roulade or Kiawe-Smoked Turkey
    - Pair with a Lilikoi Mojito or Sparkling Ginger Guava Spritz
    - Add thin-sliced avocado or pickled mango for an extra tropical layer

Roasted 'Ulu (Breadfruit) with Poke-Style Relish: Ahi, Limu & Local Chili

A modern island appetizer or side smoky roasted 'ulu topped with bright, spicy ahi poke and ocean herbs

 COOK TIME: 35 MINS   DIFFICULTY: EASY   SERVINGS: 6-8

INGREDIENTS

For the Roasted 'Ulu
- 1 medium 'ulu (breadfruit), peeled, cored, and cut into 1½-inch wedges
- 2 Tbsp macadamia nut oil or olive oil
- ½ tsp Kiawe smoked sea salt
- ¼ tsp cracked black pepper
- ½ tsp ground turmeric (optional, for color and warmth)
- 1 sprig fresh rosemary or thyme, chopped

For the Poke-Style Relish
- ½ lb. sashimi-grade ahi, cut into ¼-inch cubes
- 2 Tbsp shoyu (soy sauce or tamari)
- 1 tsp sesame oil
- 1 Tbsp finely chopped limu kohu or ogo seaweed
- ½ tsp finely minced Hawaiian chili (adjust to spice preference)
- 1 Tbsp finely diced Maui onion
- 1 tsp grated ginger
- 1 tsp lime juice
- 1 tsp toasted sesame seeds
- 1 Tbsp finely chopped green onion

For Garnish
- Extra limu or seaweed strands
- Microgreens or edible flowers ('ilima, nasturtium, or orchid petals)
- Drizzle of chili oil or macadamia nut oil

INSTRUCTIONS

Roast the 'Ulu
1. Preheat oven to 400°F (200°C).
2. Toss breadfruit wedges with oil, Kiawe smoked salt, pepper, turmeric, and herbs.
3. Spread evenly on a baking sheet lined with parchment.
4. Roast for 30–35 minutes, turning once, until golden brown and crisp on edges but creamy inside.
5. Keep warm while preparing relish.

Prepare the Poke Relish
1. In a mixing bowl, combine shoyu, sesame oil, lime juice, ginger, and chili.
2. Add ahi cubes, Maui onion, green onion, and limu.
3. Gently fold to coat evenly do not overmix.
4. Sprinkle with toasted sesame seeds.
5. Chill briefly (5–10 minutes) before serving for the freshest texture.

Assemble the Dish
1. Arrange roasted 'ulu wedges on a platter.
2. Spoon poke relish over the top or serve it alongside for DIY bites.
3. Garnish with microgreens, limu strands, and a light drizzle of chili or macadamia oil.

48

Big Island Peppered Brussels Sprouts with Bacon & Maui Onion

CHEF'S NOTES

- Local Touch: Maui onions' natural sweetness makes them ideal they caramelize without overpowering.
- Big Island Pepper Style: Use coarsely cracked pepper, not fine grind the spice is part of the texture.
- Smoky Depth: Kiawe salt or a touch of liquid smoke mimics the flavor of wood-fired 'ohana cooking.
- Make-Ahead Tip: Roast the sprouts earlier, then reheat and toss with bacon just before serving to keep them crisp.

TASTING NOTES

- Aroma: Smoky bacon and roasted vegetables with a sweet onion perfume.
- Taste: The interplay of salty, peppery bacon and sweet caramelized onion gives each bite balance and richness.
- Texture: Crisp edges, tender centers, and a satisfying crunch from bacon and macadamias.
- Pairing Ideas:
    - Serve alongside Kalua Pork Roulade or Kiawe-Smoked Turkey
    - Perfect with Poi-Mashed Potatoes and Cranberry-Pineapple Compote
    - Add a fried egg and drizzle of chili oil for a leftover brunch version

Big Island Peppered Brussels Sprouts with Bacon & Maui Onion

Crispy, smoky, and sweet a savory island-style side with bold pepper and golden caramelization

 COOK TIME: 25-30 MINS   DIFFICULTY: EASY   SERVINGS: 6-8

INGREDIENTS

For the Brussels Sprouts
- 1½ lbs Brussels sprouts, trimmed and halved
- 1 medium Maui onion, thinly sliced
- 4 slices thick-cut bacon (or turkey bacon), chopped
- 2 Tbsp olive oil or macadamia nut oil
- ½ tsp pa'akai (Hawaiian sea salt)
- 1½ tsp freshly cracked black pepper (Big Island style bold and coarse)
- ½ tsp Kiawe smoked sea salt (optional, for smoky flavor)
- 1 tsp honey or coconut nectar (optional, for balance)

For Garnish
- 1 Tbsp toasted macadamia nuts, chopped (optional)
- 1 tsp balsamic glaze or pineapple reduction drizzle
- Freshly chopped parsley or microgreens

INSTRUCTIONS

Render the Bacon
1. Heat a large oven-safe skillet (or cast iron) over medium heat.
2. Add chopped bacon and cook until golden and crisp, 5–6 minutes.
3. Remove bacon pieces with a slotted spoon, leaving about 1 Tbsp rendered fat in the pan.

Sauté the Onions
1. Add sliced Maui onion to the same pan.
2. Sauté for 2–3 minutes until translucent and lightly golden the natural sweetness enhances the savory base.

Roast the Brussels Sprouts
1. Add Brussels sprouts to the pan, cut side down. Drizzle with olive oil and season with pa'akai and coarse black pepper.
2. Transfer the skillet to a preheated oven at 400°F (200°C).
3. Roast 18–22 minutes, shaking once halfway, until sprouts are browned and tender inside with crisp edges.

Finish
1. Return bacon to the pan and toss everything together over low heat.
2. Add Kiawe smoked sea salt and a drizzle of honey (if desired) for balance.
3. Sprinkle toasted macadamia nuts and finish with a touch of balsamic or pineapple reduction for brightness.

Hawaiian Ham Glazed with Maui Pineapple

CHEF'S NOTES
- Glaze Consistency: You want it syrupy and sticky it should cling to the ham without running off.
- Local Touch: Using Maui pineapple (fresh, not canned) gives natural acidity and depth.
- Serving Suggestion: Slice thickly and serve with extra glaze on the side for dipping.
- Make-Ahead Tip: Prepare glaze 2 days ahead and rewarm gently before brushing.

TASTING NOTES
- Aroma: Roasted pineapple, brown sugar, and smoked sea salt the scent of a luau feast on Christmas morning.
- Taste: Juicy, smoky ham coated in a glossy, sweet-tart glaze with island spice heat and caramelized edges.
- Texture: Crisp on the outside, tender and moist inside, with a sticky-sweet glaze that clings beautifully.
- Pairing Ideas:
    - Serve alongside Poi-Mashed Potatoes or Lava-Rock Grilled Squash
    - Add Coconut–Pineapple Crescent Rolls to soak up extra glaze
    - Pair with Spiced Sweet Potato Casserole and a Lilikoi Spritz for the perfect island holiday meal

Hawaiian Ham Glazed with Maui Pineapple

A showstopping centerpiece glazed with tropical fruit, kissed by island spice, and roasted to golden perfection

COOK TIME: 2-2.5 HOURS ★ ★ ☆ **DIFFICULTY: MEDIUM** **SERVINGS: 10-12**

INGREDIENTS

For the Ham
- 1 whole smoked ham (8–10 lbs., bone-in preferred)
- 1 Tbsp Paia Spice Co. Blend of your choice (looking for some extra smokey add Kiawe, looking for some kick use Hela Wela)
- 1 tsp Kiawe smoked sea salt or standard Pa'akai
- Whole cloves (optional, for studding)

For the Maui Pineapple Glaze
- 1½ cups fresh pineapple juice
- ½ cup crushed or finely diced Maui pineapple
- ½ cup brown sugar or raw cane sugar
- ¼ cup local honey or macadamia nut honey
- 2 Tbsp Dijon or Hawaiian mustard
- 2 Tbsp apple cider vinegar or rice vinegar
- 1 tsp grated fresh ginger
- ½ tsp chili flakes or Paia Spice Co. Hela Wela (optional)
- 1 Tbsp butter or coconut oil (for glossy finish)

INSTRUCTIONS

Prepare the Ham
1. Preheat oven to 325°F (165°C).
2. Score the surface of the ham in a diamond pattern (about ½ inch deep).
3. Rub with Paia Spice Blend and Kiawe salt.
4. Optional: Stud the intersections of the diamonds with whole cloves for extra aroma.
5. Place ham cut side down in a roasting pan with a small rack. Add ½ cup water to the pan to keep it moist.

Make the Glaze
1. In a small saucepan, combine pineapple juice, crushed pineapple, sugar, honey, mustard, vinegar, ginger, and chili.
2. Bring to a simmer over medium heat and cook 10–12 minutes until syrupy and glossy.
3. Whisk in butter to finish for shine and flavor depth.

Glaze and Roast
1. Brush ham generously with glaze, reserving some for basting.
2. Roast uncovered for 2–2½ hours, brushing every 25–30 minutes with more glaze.
3. For a caramelized finish, increase oven to 400°F (200°C) during the last 10 minutes.
4. Remove from oven, tent with foil, and rest 15–20 minutes before slicing.

Kalua Pork Roulade with Hawaiian-Style Crackling & Molokai Sweet Potatoes

CHEF'S NOTES

- Authentic Smoke: For true imu-style depth, wrap the seasoned roulade in ti leaves or banana leaves before roasting it will gently steam and perfume the meat.
- Crisp Skin Secret: Leaving the pork uncovered overnight dries the skin for maximum crackling.
- Purple 'Uala: Molokai sweet potatoes not only bring stunning color but also an earthy sweetness that complements the smoky pork.
- Make-Ahead: Roulade can be prepped and rolled a day early simply roast day-of.
- Variation: Substitute pork shoulder for a leaner, more traditional Kalua pork texture.

TASTING NOTES

- Aroma: Roasted pork and kiawe smoke with hints of garlic, herbs, and toasted salt like a luau feast in the oven.
- Taste: Deeply savory and smoky with balanced sweetness from ʻuala and caramelized drippings. The herbs add freshness, while the crackling gives irresistible crunch.
- Texture: Crisp outer layer, juicy interior, melt-in-your-mouth tenderness.
  - Pairing Ideas:
  - Serve with Cranberry-Pineapple Compote for a sweet-tart contrast
  - Add Poi-Mashed Potatoes or Lava-Rock Grilled Squash for a complete Hawaiian holiday spread
  - Drizzle lightly with Lilikoi Gravy or Pineapple Gastrique for a bright finish

Kalua Pork Roulade with Hawaiian-Style Crackling & Molokai Sweet Potatoes

A modern luau feasts smoky, juicy pork rolled with herbs, roasted to crisp perfection, and served with caramelized island 'uala

 COOK TIME: 3-3.5 HOURS   DIFFICULTY: HARD   SERVINGS: 8-10

INGREDIENTS

For the Pork Roulade
- 1 boneless pork belly (about 3½–4 lbs.), skin on
- 1½ Tbsp Kiawe smoked sea salt
- 2 tsp Hawaiian sea salt (Pa'akai)
- 1 Tbsp brown sugar or coconut sugar
- 1 Tbsp minced garlic
- 1 Tbsp fresh ginger, grated
- 2 Tbsp macadamia nut oil
- 2 tsp liquid smoke (or optional wrap in ti leaves and bake for traditional flavor)
- 1 Tbsp chopped fresh rosemary
- 1 Tbsp chopped thyme
- 1 Tbsp chopped parsley
- 2 green onions, finely chopped
- Freshly ground black pepper to taste

For the Molokai Sweet Potatoes
- 2 lbs. purple Molokai 'uala (or orange sweet potatoes), peeled and cubed
- 2 Tbsp coconut oil or olive oil
- 1 Tbsp honey or maple syrup
- ½ tsp Pa'akai
- 1 Tbsp fresh lime juice
- 1 Tbsp chopped fresh mint or cilantro (optional for garnish)

INSTRUCTIONS

Prepare the Pork Belly
1. Lay pork belly skin-side down on a cutting board. Score the flesh slightly in a crosshatch pattern (not through the skin).
2. In a small bowl, mix Kiawe smoked salt, Pa'akai, brown sugar, garlic, ginger, herbs, green onion, and macadamia oil into a paste.
3. Rub mixture thoroughly over the meat (underside only), massaging it into the cuts.
4. Roll pork belly tightly into a log (skin outside) and secure with kitchen twine every 1½ inches.
5. Place uncovered in the fridge overnight to dry the skin and let flavors penetrate.

Roast the Roulade
1. Preheat oven to 300°F (150°C).
2. Place the roulade on a roasting rack in a baking pan.
3. Roast for 2½–3 hours, basting occasionally with pan drippings.
4. For crackling finish: increase oven temperature to 450°F (230°C) for the final 20–25 minutes until skin is blistered and crisp.
5. Rest 15–20 minutes before slicing.

Roast the Molokai Sweet Potatoes
1. While the pork roasts, toss 'uala cubes with oil, honey, and salt.
2. Spread on a baking sheet and roast at 400°F (200°C) for 25–30 minutes until tender and caramelized.
3. Toss with lime juice and herbs just before serving for brightness.

Molasses Gingerbread Haupia Cupcakes

CHEF'S NOTES

- Haupia Texture: You want it silky and thick enough to hold shape, like a pudding-meets-whipped cream hybrid.
- Island Touch: A splash of rum or Kona coffee extract in the batter makes this next level.
- Make-Ahead: Bake cupcakes one day ahead; frost day-of for freshness. Haupia can be refrigerated up to 2 days.
- Serving Tip: Chill briefly before serving for the best flavor contrast cool frosting, warm spices.

TASTING NOTES

- Aroma: Holiday spice with toasted coconut and a whisper of molasses warm yet tropical.
- Taste: Deep, dark gingerbread flavor balanced by creamy coconut sweetness. Every bite is cozy but bright.
- Texture: Soft, tender crumb meets silky-smooth haupia a luxurious, melt-in-your-mouth finish.
- Pairing Ideas:
    - Serve after Kalua Pork Roulade or Kiawe-Smoked Turkey
    - Pair with Kona Coffee or Spiced Coconut Chai
    - Add gold dust or orchid petals for a holiday presentation worthy of a luau-style celebration

Molasses Gingerbread Haupia Cupcakes

Spiced holiday cupcakes topped with cool coconut pudding cream the perfect tropical Christmas fusion

 COOK TIME: 20-22 MINS   DIFFICULTY: EASY   SERVINGS: 12

INGREDIENTS

For the Gingerbread Cupcakes
- 1¾ cups all-purpose flour
- 1 tsp baking soda
- ½ tsp baking powder
- ½ tsp Pa'akai (Hawaiian sea salt)
- 1½ tsp ground ginger
- 1 tsp ground cinnamon
- ½ tsp nutmeg
- ¼ tsp ground cloves
- ½ cup unsalted butter, softened
- ½ cup brown sugar
- ½ cup molasses (dark, unsulfured)
- 1 large egg
- ½ cup buttermilk (or coconut milk + 1 tsp vinegar for dairy-free version)
- 1 tsp vanilla extract

For the Haupia (Coconut Pudding) Frosting
- 1 cup full-fat coconut milk
- 1 cup water
- ½ cup sugar
- ¼ cup cornstarch
- 1 tsp vanilla extract
- Pinch of Pa'akai
- ½ cup heavy cream or whipped coconut cream (for blending)

Optional Garnish
Toasted coconut flakes | Crystallized ginger pieces | Sprinkle of cinnamon or nutmeg | Edible gold or

INSTRUCTIONS

Make the Gingerbread Cupcakes

1. Preheat oven to 350°F (175°C). Line a 12-cup muffin tin with cupcake liners.
2. In a medium bowl, whisk flour, baking soda, baking powder, salt, and all spices.
3. In a large bowl, cream butter and brown sugar until fluffy.
4. Add molasses, egg, vanilla, and buttermilk, mix until smooth.
5. Gradually add dry ingredients, mixing just until combined.
6. Fill cupcake liners about ¾ full.
7. Bake 20–22 minutes or until a toothpick comes out clean.
8. Cool completely on a wire rack.

Prepare the Haupia Frosting

1. In a saucepan, whisk coconut milk, water, sugar, cornstarch, and salt.
2. Cook over medium heat, stirring constantly, until thickened (about 5–7 minutes).
3. Remove from heat, stir in vanilla, and let cool completely.
4. Once cooled, fold in whipped cream or whipped coconut cream until light and fluffy.
5. Chill 15 minutes before frosting.

Assemble

1. Swirl haupia frosting over cooled cupcakes using a piping bag or spoon.
2. Garnish with toasted coconut, crystallized ginger, or a dusting of cinnamon.

Christmas Spice 'Uala (Sweet Potato) Pie with Kiawe-Smoked Sea Salt Crust

CHEF'S NOTES

- Kiawe Salt Magic: The smoky mineral note transforms the crust it's subtle but adds depth that balances sweetness beautifully.
- 'Uala Choice: Molokai purple 'uala gives a stunning color and slightly nutty flavor; orange sweet potatoes give a classic golden look.
- Texture Tip: Don't overbake the pie should be silky and custard-like, not dry.
- Make-Ahead: Bake the day before and chill overnight; it slices cleaner and the flavors develop beautifully.

TASTING NOTES

- Aroma: Toasted coconut, caramelized 'uala, warm cinnamon, and a whisper of island smoke.
- Taste: Sweet and spiced like pumpkin pie but with deeper, earthier notes and a hint of savory from Kiawe salt.
- Texture: Velvety smooth filling with a flaky, buttery crust each bite melts into smoky sweetness.
- Pairing Ideas:
    - Serve with Hibiscus–Cranberry Mocktail or Kona Coffee
    - Complements Kiawe-Smoked Turkey or Kalua Pork Roulade beautifully on the holiday table
    - Add a drizzle of Salted Caramel Coconut Sauce for a decadent finish

Christmas Spice 'Uala (Sweet Potato) Pie with Kiawe-Smoked Sea Salt Crust

Silky roasted 'uala filling, warm island spices, and a golden, smoky-salted crust a Hawaiian twist on a holiday classic

 COOK TIME: 55-65 MINS   ★ DIFFICULTY: MEDIUM   SERVINGS: 8

INGREDIENTS

For the Kiawe-Smoked Sea Salt Crust
- 1¼ cups all-purpose flour
- ¼ cup finely ground macadamia nuts (optional for texture)
- ½ tsp Kiawe smoked sea salt
- 1 Tbsp sugar
- ½ cup (1 stick) cold unsalted butter, cubed
- 3–4 Tbsp ice-cold water

For the 'Uala Filling
- 2 cups mashed roasted 'uala (Hawaiian sweet potato, purple or orange variety)
- ¾ cup brown sugar
- ½ cup coconut milk (full fat)
- 2 eggs, lightly beaten
- 2 Tbsp melted butter or coconut oil
- 1 tsp vanilla extract
- 1 tsp ground cinnamon
- ½ tsp ground ginger
- ¼ tsp nutmeg
- ¼ tsp allspice
- Pinch of Pa'akai (Hawaiian sea salt)
- Optional: 1 Tbsp rum or bourbon for depth

For Garnish
- Coconut whipped cream or vanilla Chantilly
- Sprinkle of Kiawe smoked sea salt or cinnamon
- Toasted coconut flakes or crushed macadamia nuts

INSTRUCTIONS

Make the Crust
1. In a bowl, whisk flour, sugar, and Kiawe smoked salt.
2. Cut in butter with a pastry cutter or fingers until coarse crumbs form.
3. Add ice water 1 Tbsp at a time, mixing until dough just comes together.
4. Shape into a disc, wrap, and chill for 30 minutes.
5. Roll out to fit a 9-inch pie pan. Trim edges and crimp decoratively.
6. Prebake at 375°F (190°C) for 10 minutes with pie weights. Cool slightly.

Prepare the 'Uala Filling
1. Roast whole sweet potatoes at 400°F (200°C) until tender (about 45 minutes), then peel and mash.
2. In a bowl, combine mashed 'uala, brown sugar, coconut milk, eggs, butter, vanilla, and spices.
3. Whisk until smooth and creamy.

Assemble & Bake
1. Pour filling into cooled crust and smooth the top.
2. Bake at 350°F (175°C) for 45–50 minutes, or until the center is set but slightly jiggly.
3. Cool completely on a wire rack before slicing.

Serve
Top with a dollop of coconut whipped cream, a sprinkle of smoked salt, and toasted coconut flakes for texture and sparkle.

Spam Musubi Sliders with Teriyaki Glaze & Pickled Maui Onion

CHEF'S NOTES
- Rice Matters: Slightly warm, sticky sushi rice holds its shape best, not freshly steamed or too dry.
- Spam Upgrade: Try Spam Lite or Teri Spam for a different flavor; searing creates the perfect crispy edge.
- Pickled Onions: The sweetness of Maui onions and acidity of rice vinegar balance the glaze's richness beautifully.
- Serving Style: These sliders make excellent holiday appetizers, bite-sized, portable, and irresistibly glossy.

TASTING NOTES
- Aroma: Sweet soy caramel, toasted seaweed, and tropical pineapple with a savory edge.
- Taste: A perfect harmony of salty-sweet Spam, tangy onions, and umami glaze, lifted by the freshness of the rice.
- Texture: Crisp exterior, soft rice interior, and crunchy, bright onion bite.
- Color: Golden Spam, ruby onion, white rice, and glossy nori, like a tiny island feast in every piece.

Spam Musubi Sliders with Teriyaki Glaze & Pickled Maui Onion

Mini island sliders layered with crispy seared Spam, teriyaki glaze, sushi rice, and tangy pickled onions, Hawai'i's favorite snack reimagined for the holidays

COOK TIME: 20 MINS   ★ ★ ★ **DIFFICULTY: EASY**   **SERVINGS: 12**

INGREDIENTS

For the Spam
- 1 can classic Spam (12 oz), cut into 12 slices
- 1 Tbsp soy sauce or tamari
- 1 Tbsp brown sugar
- 1 Tbsp pineapple juice
- ½ tsp grated ginger

For the Teriyaki Glaze
- ¼ cup soy sauce
- 2 Tbsp mirin or rice wine
- 2 Tbsp brown sugar or honey
- 1 Tbsp pineapple juice
- 1 tsp minced garlic
- ½ tsp cornstarch + 1 tsp water (slurry for thickening)

For the Pickled Maui Onions
- 1 medium Maui onion, thinly sliced
- ½ cup rice vinegar
- ¼ cup water
- 2 Tbsp sugar
- ½ tsp pa'akai (Hawaiian sea salt)
- Optional: pinch of chili flakes or few pink peppercorns

For the Rice Slider "Buns"
- 3 cups cooked short-grain sushi rice, slightly cooled
- 1 Tbsp rice vinegar
- 1 tsp sugar
- ½ tsp salt
- 1 sheet nori (seaweed), cut into small strips

Optional Toppings
- Toasted sesame seeds
- Avocado slices
- Thin cucumber rounds
- Furikake seasoning

INSTRUCTIONS

Pickle the Onions
1. Combine vinegar, water, sugar, salt, and chili in a small saucepan. Bring to a light simmer.
2. Pour hot mixture over sliced onions in a jar.
3. Cool to room temperature, then refrigerate for at least 1 hour (or overnight for deeper flavor).

Make the Teriyaki Glaze
1. In a small saucepan, combine soy sauce, mirin, brown sugar, pineapple juice, and garlic.
2. Simmer over medium heat for 5–7 minutes.
3. Stir in cornstarch slurry; cook until thickened and glossy.
4. Remove from heat and set aside.

Cook the Spam
1. Mix soy sauce, brown sugar, pineapple juice, and ginger in a small bowl.
2. Pan-sear Spam slices over medium-high heat until golden and caramelized (1–2 minutes per side).
3. Brush with teriyaki glaze while still hot.

Shape the Rice Buns
1. Mix rice with vinegar, sugar, and salt.
2. Using damp hands or a musubi mold, form into small rectangles or circles (about 2 inches wide).
3. Sear lightly on one side in a nonstick pan to crisp the surface slightly, if desired.

Assemble the Sliders
1. Place a slice of teriyaki-glazed Spam on one rice patty.
2. Add a few pickled onion rings and optional toppings like avocado or cucumber.
3. Top with another rice patty.
4. Wrap a thin strip of nori around the slider to hold it together.
5. Brush with a final drizzle of teriyaki glaze/sprinkle with sesame seeds.

Charred Taro Leaf Wraps Filled with Seasonal Vegetables and Island Spice

CHEF'S NOTES

- Laua'o Care: Always cook taro leaves before eating, raw leaves contain calcium oxalate crystals that must be neutralized by heat.
- Flavor Harmony: The turmeric and ginger evoke imu-style (underground oven) warmth; coconut milk adds creaminess that ties everything together.
- Make It a Feast: Pair with Poi-Mashed Potatoes, Coconut Rice & Black Beans, or 'Ilima Bread Stuffing for a complete plant-based holiday spread.
- Presentation Tip: Slice diagonally and arrange on a platter with tropical flowers or banana leaves for a luau-inspired look.

TASTING NOTES

- Aroma: Roasted vegetables, coconut, and gentle smoke, reminiscent of a traditional imu fire pit.
- Taste: Earthy, spiced, and slightly sweet with a creamy, savory finish. The lime and herbs brighten each bite.
- Texture: Tender, smoky taro leaves encasing soft, flavorful vegetables, comforting yet refined.
- Color: Deep green exterior with vibrant orange, gold, and red filling, a beautiful, natural mosaic.

Charred Taro Leaf Wraps Filled with Seasonal Vegetables & Island Spice

Smoky, tender taro leaves encase a colorful filling of roasted island vegetables, coconut, and aromatic herbs, a plant-based celebration of aloha

COOK TIME: 35-40 MINS   ★ ★ ☆ DIFFICULTY: MEDIUM   SERVINGS: 6

INGREDIENTS

For the Wraps
- 12 medium taro (laua'o) leaves, stems trimmed
- 1 Tbsp macadamia nut oil or coconut oil
- Pinch of pa'akai (Hawaiian sea salt)

For the Filling
- 1 cup diced 'uala (sweet potato)
- 1 cup diced kabocha squash or butternut squash
- ½ cup diced Maui onion
- ½ cup diced red bell pepper
- ½ cup diced zucchini
- 2 cloves garlic, minced
- 1 tsp grated fresh ginger
- ½ tsp turmeric
- ½ tsp ground coriander
- 1 tsp Paia Spice Co. Island Blend (or substitute chili, smoked paprika & allspice mix)
- ¼ cup coconut milk (to bind)
- 1 Tbsp soy sauce or tamari
- 1 Tbsp lime juice
- ¼ cup chopped fresh cilantro or parsley

Optional Garnishes
- Toasted coconut flakes
- Crispy fried onions
- Microgreens or edible flowers

INSTRUCTIONS

Prepare the Taro Leaves
1. Rinse and pat dry the taro leaves.
2. Steam or blanch leaves for 3–4 minutes until pliable and glossy green (this removes natural bitterness).
3. Lay flat on a towel to cool. Brush lightly with macadamia nut oil and sprinkle with pa'akai.

Make the Filling
1. Preheat oven to 400°F (200°C).
2. Toss all diced vegetables with a little oil, salt, and spice blend.
3. Roast on a parchment-lined tray for 15–20 minutes until tender and slightly caramelized.
4. In a large bowl, combine roasted veggies with garlic, ginger, coconut milk, soy sauce, lime juice, and herbs. Mix to a moist, cohesive filling.

Assemble the Wraps
1. Place two overlapping taro leaves (shiny side down) on your work surface.
2. Spoon about 1/3 cup of filling into the center.
3. Fold sides inward, then roll up like a burrito to seal.
4. Repeat until all filling is used.

Cook the Wraps

Option 1 Oven-Baked:
1. Place wraps seam-side down in a lightly oiled baking dish.
2. Cover with foil and bake for 20 minutes at 375°F.
3. Uncover and broil briefly to lightly char the tops for a smoky finish.

Option 2 — Grill or Pan-Sear:
1. Grill each wrap 2–3 minutes per side until charred and aromatic.
2. Serve warm with a drizzle of coconut-lime sauce or chili oil.

Lava Rock Grilled Skewers: Chicken, Pineapple & Bell Pepper

CHEF'S NOTES

- Lava Rock Magic: Grilling over lava rock retains heat evenly and imparts that distinct, smoky sear reminiscent of traditional imu cooking.
- Pineapple Caramelization: Maui Gold pineapple is ideal, high in natural sugar, it caramelizes into a golden glaze as it grills.
- Marinade Variations: Add 1 Tbsp coconut milk for richness. Swap chicken for tofu or shrimp for variety. A splash of rum in the marinade adds depth and holiday flair.
- Make It a Platter: Add grilled zucchini, mushrooms, or cherry tomatoes for more color and texture.

TASTING NOTE'S

- Aroma: Smoky soy, caramelized pineapple, and a hint of ginger-lime, pure island BBQ perfume.
- Taste: Sweet and tangy glaze balances savory chicken and roasted peppers; sea salt adds that last perfect sparkle.
- Texture: Juicy and tender with crisp caramelized edges; pineapple bursts with juicy sweetness.
- Color: Golden brown, crimson red, and sunny yellow, like a Hawaiian sunset on a skewer.

Lava Rock Grilled Skewers: Chicken, Pineapple & Bell Pepper

Juicy marinated chicken skewers grilled over lava rock heat with caramelized pineapple and bright island veggies, the taste of aloha BBQ

 COOK TIME: 10-12 MINS   ★ DIFFICULTY: EASY   SERVINGS: 6

INGREDIENTS

For the Marinade
- ¼ cup soy sauce or tamari
- 2 Tbsp brown sugar or local honey
- 2 Tbsp pineapple juice
- 1 Tbsp rice vinegar or apple cider vinegar
- 1 Tbsp grated fresh ginger
- 1 clove garlic, minced
- 1 tsp sesame oil or macadamia nut oil
- ½ tsp chili flakes (optional for heat)
- 1 tsp lime zest

For the Skewers
- 1½ lbs boneless, skinless chicken thighs or breast, cut into 1½-inch cubes
- 2 cups fresh pineapple chunks
- 2 red or yellow bell peppers, cut into 1½-inch pieces
- 1 small Maui onion, cut into wedges
- Macadamia nut oil or olive oil, for brushing
- Pa'akai (Hawaiian sea salt), to finish

For Garnish
- Chopped green onions or cilantro
- Toasted sesame seeds
- Lime wedges

INSTRUCTIONS

Marinate the Chicken
1. Whisk together all marinade ingredients in a bowl.
2. Add chicken pieces, toss to coat, and cover.
3. Marinate for at least 1 hour (or up to overnight) in the refrigerator.

Assemble the Skewers
1. Thread marinated chicken, pineapple, bell pepper, and onion alternately onto skewers.
2. Brush lightly with oil for extra caramelization.
3. If using wooden skewers, soak them in water for 20 minutes beforehand to prevent burning.

Grill over Lava Rock or BBQ
1. Preheat grill or lava rock surface to medium-high heat (about 400°F / 200°C).
2. Grill skewers for 4–5 minutes per side, brushing occasionally with remaining marinade until chicken is cooked through and nicely charred.
3. Sprinkle lightly with pa'akai just before removing from heat.

Serve
Arrange on a platter, sprinkle with green onions and sesame seeds, and serve with lime wedges for brightness.
They can also be served over Coconut Rice or alongside 'Ilima Bread Stuffing for a festive plate.

Coconut Rice & Black Beans Bowl with Island Herbs

CHEF'S NOTES

- Good Luck Inspiration: Black beans represent prosperity, coconut symbolizes cleansing and new beginnings, and rice stands for abundance, all in one island-style bowl.
- Flavor Balance: The trick is restraint, let the herbs and coconut milk shine without overpowering with spice.
- Make It Heartier: Add roasted 'uala cubes or grilled mahi mahi for a complete meal.
- Make Ahead: Cook the rice and beans separately a day in advance; reheat gently with a splash of coconut milk before serving.

TASTING NOTES

- Aroma: Tropical coconut steam mingles with warm herbs and citrus zest.
- Taste: Comforting and layered, sweet coconut cream, earthy beans, bright lime, and fresh green herbs.
- Texture: Soft, creamy rice with tender beans and the pop of fresh herbs.
- Color: Ivory rice, deep black beans, and vibrant greens, a simple but stunning bowl of abundance.

Coconut Rice & Black Beans "Lucky Grains" Bowl with Island Herbs

Creamy coconut rice and hearty black beans with a vibrant mix of tropical herbs, a wholesome, symbolic start to the new year

 COOK TIME: 30 MINS   DIFFICULTY: EASY   SERVINGS: 4-6

INGREDIENTS

For the Coconut Rice
- 1½ cups jasmine or long-grain rice
- 1½ cups coconut milk (full-fat)
- 1¼ cups water
- 1 Tbsp coconut oil or butter
- ½ tsp pa'akai (Hawaiian sea salt)
- 1 pandan leaf or 1 kaffir lime leaf (optional, for aroma)

For the Black Beans
- 2 cups cooked black beans (or 1 can, drained and rinsed)
- 1 Tbsp macadamia nut oil or olive oil
- 1 small Maui onion, finely chopped
- 2 cloves garlic, minced
- ½ tsp ground cumin
- ¼ tsp allspice
- ¼ tsp black pepper
- 1 Tbsp lime juice
- ¼ cup coconut milk (to finish)
- Pa'akai to taste

For the Island Herb Mix
- 2 Tbsp chopped fresh cilantro
- 1 Tbsp chopped green onion
- 1 Tbsp chopped parsley or cilantro (if available)
- 1 tsp minced fresh basil or Thai basil
- 1 tsp minced fresh mint (optional, for brightness)
- Zest of ½ lime

INSTRUCTIONS

Cook the Coconut Rice
1. Rinse rice until water runs clear.
2. In a saucepan, combine rice, coconut milk, water, coconut oil, salt, and pandan or lime leaf (if using).
3. Bring to a gentle boil, then cover and reduce heat to low.
4. Simmer 15 minutes, then let rest (covered) for another 10 minutes.
5. Fluff gently with a fork. Remove leaf before serving.

Prepare the Black Beans
1. Heat oil in a pan over medium heat. Add onion and sauté until translucent.
2. Add garlic, cumin, allspice, and pepper; cook 1 minute more.
3. Stir in black beans, lime juice, and coconut milk.
4. Simmer 5–7 minutes, stirring occasionally, until creamy and fragrant.
5. Adjust salt and lime to taste.

Make the Island Herb Mix
1. Combine all chopped herbs, lime zest, and a small pinch of sea salt in a bowl.
2. Toss lightly to blend.

Assemble the "Lucky Grains" Bowl
1. Spoon a base of coconut rice into each bowl.
2. Top with a generous helping of black beans.
3. Sprinkle with the island herb mix and your choice of garnishes (avocado, coconut flakes, papaya, etc.).
4. Finish with a light drizzle of lime vinaigrette or chili oil for contrast.

Island-Style Hoppin' John:
Black-Eyed Peas, Gochujang Island Spice & Coconut Rice

CHEF'S NOTES
- Fusion Inspiration: This recipe honors Hoppin' John's symbolism of luck and prosperity, blending it with Hawai'i's multicultural spirit. Gochujang adds a savory-sweet depth that complements coconut beautifully.
- Texture Tip: Don't over-reduce the beans, they should be creamy and slightly saucy, like a tropical stew.
- Variations:
    - Add diced Portuguese sausage or smoked tofu for richness.
    - Stir in chopped kale or spinach during the last few minutes for color and nutrition.
    - For extra heat, drizzle with chili oil or Hawaiian chili pepper water before serving.
- Make-Ahead: The flavors deepen overnight, perfect for prepping ahead for New Year's Day.

TASTING NOTES
- Aroma: Toasted coconut, smoky chili, and sweet onions, comforting yet exotic.
- Taste: A creamy harmony of spice, sweetness, and umami with bright lime and herb lift.
- Texture: Silky coconut rice meets tender beans, soft, rich, and deeply satisfying.
- Color: Fiery orange-red beans over ivory coconut rice, sprinkled with tropical greens, festive and inviting.

Island-Style Hoppin' John:
Black-Eyed Peas, Gochujang Island Spice & Coconut Rice

A soulful, spicy-sweet twist on a Southern classic, black-eyed peas tossed in gochujang and coconut cream over fragrant island rice

 COOK TIME: 30 MINS   DIFFICULTY: EASY   SERVINGS: 6

INGREDIENTS

For the Coconut Rice
- 1½ cups jasmine or basmati rice
- 1½ cups coconut milk (full-fat)
- 1¼ cups water
- 1 Tbsp coconut oil or butter
- ½ tsp pa'akai (Hawaiian sea salt)
- 1 pandan or kaffir lime leaf (optional, for aroma)

For the Black-Eyed Peas
- 2 cups cooked black-eyed peas (or 1 can, drained and rinsed)
- 1 Tbsp macadamia nut oil or olive oil
- ½ cup diced Maui onion
- 2 cloves garlic, minced
- ½ tsp grated ginger
- 1 Tbsp gochujang (Korean chili paste, adjust to spice level)
- 1 tsp soy sauce or tamari
- ½ tsp rice vinegar or lime juice
- ¼ cup coconut milk
- ½ cup diced bell pepper (red or yellow)
- ½ tsp smoked paprika (optional)
- Fresh-cracked black pepper to taste

For the Island Herb Mix
- ¼ cup chopped fresh cilantro
- 2 Tbsp chopped green onions
- 1 tsp lime zest
- 1 Tbsp toasted shredded coconut (optional for garnish)

INSTRUCTIONS

Cook the Coconut Rice
1. Rinse rice until the water runs clear.
2. In a medium pot, combine rice, coconut milk, water, coconut oil, and salt (plus pandan leaf if using).
3. Bring to a gentle boil, cover, and reduce heat to low.
4. Simmer 15 minutes, then remove from heat and let steam (covered) for 10 minutes.
5. Fluff gently with a fork.

Prepare the Black-Eyed Peas
1. In a large skillet, heat oil over medium heat.
2. Add onion and sauté 3–4 minutes until translucent.
3. Stir in garlic, ginger, and gochujang; cook 1 minute to release aroma.
4. Add black-eyed peas, soy sauce, vinegar, coconut milk, and bell pepper.
5. Simmer 10 minutes, stirring gently, until beans are creamy and infused with spice.
6. Adjust seasoning with salt, pepper, or lime juice to balance richness.

Assemble the Island Hoppin' John
1. Spoon warm coconut rice into a large bowl or serving platter.
2. Top generously with the black-eyed pea mixture.
3. Sprinkle with the island herb mix and toasted coconut.
4. Serve hot, perfect as a standalone bowl or side to grilled fish, chicken, or tofu.

Pineapple–Ginger Glazed Pork Tenderloin with Roasted Kukui Nut–Herb Crumbs

CHEF'S NOTES

- Kukui Nuts: Traditional to Hawai'i, these nuts add buttery richness and a gentle smokiness. Toast them lightly, they burn fast!
- Pineapple Variety: Choose Maui Gold for its sweetness and low acidity.
- Make It a Feast: Serve with Poi-Mashed Potatoes or Charred Laua'o Beans for a balanced island plate.
- Make-Ahead Tip: Glaze and crumb mixture can be prepared one day ahead; just sear and roast fresh for best texture.

TASTING NOTES

- Aroma: Sweet roasted pineapple mingles with ginger and nutty warmth, tropical yet refined.
- Taste: Caramelized glaze balances tang and sweetness; herbs and nuts bring texture and savory depth.
- Texture: Juicy tenderloin with glossy glaze and a crunchy, buttery crumb finish.
- Color: Deep golds and ambers with a hint of green from fresh herbs, a visual celebration of abundance.

Pineapple–Ginger Glazed Pork Tenderloin with Roasted Kukui Nut–Herb Crumbs

Tender roasted pork with a golden pineapple glaze, perfumed with ginger and topped with crunchy island nut-herb crumbs

 COOK TIME: 30-35 MINS   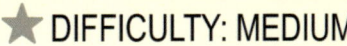 DIFFICULTY: MEDIUM    SERVINGS: 6

INGREDIENTS

For the Pork
- 2 pork tenderloins (about 2½ lbs total)
- 2 Tbsp macadamia nut oil or olive oil
- 1½ tsp pa'akai (Hawaiian sea salt)
- ½ tsp black pepper
- ½ tsp ground coriander
- 1 Tbsp fresh ginger, grated
- 1 clove garlic, minced

For the Pineapple–Ginger Glaze
- ¾ cup pineapple juice
- ¼ cup finely diced fresh pineapple
- 2 Tbsp brown sugar or local honey
- 1 Tbsp rice vinegar or apple cider vinegar
- 1 Tbsp soy sauce or tamari
- 1 tsp grated fresh ginger
- ½ tsp cornstarch + 1 tsp water (optional, to thicken)
- 1 tsp butter or coconut oil (to finish)

For the Roasted Kukui Nut–Herb Crumbs
- ¼ cup toasted kukui nuts (or macadamias if unavailable)
- 1 slice day-old bread or ¼ cup panko breadcrumbs
- 1 tsp fresh thyme or oregano, chopped
- 1 tsp fresh parsley or cilantro, chopped
- Zest of ½ lime
- Pinch of pa'akai and pepper

Optional Garnish
- Pineapple slices (grilled or roasted)
- Microgreens or edible flowers

INSTRUCTIONS

Prepare and Sear the Pork
1. Preheat oven to 400°F (200°C).
2. Pat pork dry and season with salt, pepper, coriander, garlic, and ginger.
3. Heat oil in an ovenproof skillet over medium-high heat.
4. Sear pork on all sides until golden brown (about 2–3 minutes per side).
5. Remove from heat and set aside while making glaze.

Make the Pineapple–Ginger Glaze
1. In a small saucepan, combine pineapple juice, diced pineapple, brown sugar, vinegar, soy sauce, and ginger.
2. Bring to a simmer and cook 8–10 minutes until reduced by about one-third.
3. If you prefer a thicker glaze, stir in cornstarch slurry and cook 1–2 minutes more.
4. Remove from heat and whisk in butter or coconut oil for gloss.

Roast and Glaze
1. Brush pork generously with glaze and transfer skillet to oven.
2. Roast 15–20 minutes, brushing with glaze halfway through, until internal temperature reaches 145°F (63°C).
3. Remove from oven, tent loosely with foil, and rest 10 minutes before slicing.

Make the Roasted Kukui Nut–Herb Crumbs
1. Pulse toasted kukui nuts and bread (or panko) in a food processor until coarse crumbs form.
2. Mix with chopped herbs, lime zest, salt, and pepper.
3. Toast mixture in a dry skillet or oven (350°F / 175°C) for 4–5 minutes until fragrant and golden.

Assemble
1. Slice pork tenderloin into medallions and arrange on a platter.
2. Drizzle with extra pineapple glaze.
3. Sprinkle generously with roasted nut–herb crumbs for crunch and aroma.
4. Garnish with grilled pineapple or microgreens.

Macadamia-Crusted Mahi Mahi with Mango–Papaya Salsa

CHEF'S NOTES
- Fish Freshness: Mahi mahi should be firm, pinkish, and mildly sweet, not fishy. You can substitute ono or opakapaka if desired.
- Macadamia Tip: Toast nuts lightly before chopping for extra aroma and crunch.
- Coconut Accent: The touch of coconut milk in the egg wash helps the crust brown beautifully and adds subtle island richness.
- Make It Saucy: For a luxe twist, drizzle with a thin coconut-lime beurre blanc or honey-ginger glaze.

TASTING NOTES
- Aroma: Buttery seared fish, toasted macadamias, and bright citrus.
- Taste: Sweet tropical fruit balanced by savory crust and gentle sea salt.
- Texture: Crisp crust, tender flaky fish, juicy fresh salsa, layered perfection.
- Color: Vibrant golds, pinks, and greens, the palette of a Maui sunset.

Macadamia-Crusted Mahi Mahi with Mango–Papaya Salsa

Buttery island fish, crisp macadamia crust, and a burst of tropical fruit, a bright and luxurious Hawaiian main dish for the holidays

⏱ COOK TIME: 15 MINS ★ ★ ☆ DIFFICULTY: MEDIUM 🍴 SERVINGS: 4

INGREDIENTS

For the Mahi Mahi
- 4 fresh mahi mahi fillets (6 oz each)
- ½ cup finely chopped roasted macadamia nuts
- ¼ cup panko breadcrumbs
- 2 Tbsp all-purpose flour (or tapioca flour for gluten-free)
- 1 large egg, beaten
- 1 Tbsp coconut milk
- ½ tsp pa'akai (Hawaiian sea salt)
- ¼ tsp freshly ground black pepper
- 2 Tbsp macadamia nut oil or neutral oil (for searing)
- 1 Tbsp butter or coconut oil (for finishing)

For the Mango–Papaya Salsa
- ½ cup ripe mango, diced
- ½ cup ripe papaya, diced
- 2 Tbsp red bell pepper, diced
- 2 Tbsp Maui onion, finely minced
- 1 Tbsp fresh lime juice
- 1 tsp honey or agave
- 1 Tbsp fresh cilantro or mint, chopped
- Pinch of chili flakes or minced Hawaiian chili (optional)
- Pinch of pa'akai

Optional Garnish
- Microgreens or cilantro sprigs
- Lime wedges
- Toasted coconut flakes

INSTRUCTIONS

Prepare the Salsa
1. In a small bowl, combine mango, papaya, bell pepper, onion, lime juice, honey, herbs, and chili (if using).
2. Season lightly with pa'akai.
3. Stir gently, cover, and chill until serving to let flavors meld.

Crust the Mahi Mahi
1. Pat fillets dry and season with salt and pepper.
2. In one bowl, mix flour and panko. In another, combine macadamia nuts. In a third, whisk egg and coconut milk.
3. Dredge each fillet lightly in flour mixture, dip in egg wash, then press into the macadamia mixture to coat evenly.
4. Place coated fillets on a parchment-lined plate and chill for 10 minutes to help the crust set.

Cook the Fish
1. Heat macadamia nut oil in a skillet over medium-high heat.
2. Add mahi mahi fillets and sear 3–4 minutes per side, until golden and crusted.
3. Lower heat, add butter, and baste gently for a nutty, aromatic finish.
4. Fish should flake easily but remain moist inside.

Assemble & Serve
1. Spoon a generous portion of chilled mango–papaya salsa over or beside each fillet.
2. Garnish with microgreens, toasted coconut, and a squeeze of lime.
3. Serve immediately, this dish shines brightest fresh from the pan.

Champagne Mango Float Dessert with Coconut Whip

CHEF'S NOTES

- Sparkling Choice: Champagne adds sophistication and crisp acidity; sparkling guava soda keeps it family-friendly and fragrant.
- Make It Ahead: Assemble up to a day in advance, the sponge soaks in flavor beautifully overnight.
- Texture Tip: The goal is creamy yet buoyant, the bubbles and fruit make it feel celebratory, not heavy.
- Flavor Variations:
  - Add passion fruit pulp for extra tang.
  - Layer in toasted macadamias for crunch.
  - Use pineapple instead of papaya for a brighter citrus tone.

TASTING NOTES

- Aroma: Fresh tropical fruit, coconut cream, and faint effervescence.
- Taste: Creamy coconut meets bright mango and lime, uplifted by the sparkle of guava or champagne.
- Texture: Soft sponge soaked in bubbles, silky cream, and juicy fruit, every bite melts and fizzes slightly.
- Color: Golden mango, coral papaya, white coconut, radiant and sunlit, like a Maui morning.

Champagne Mango Float Dessert with Coconut Whip

A festive island parfait, layers of mango, sponge, coconut cream, and a hint of guava or champagne sparkle

⏱ COOK TIME: 25 MINS ★ ☆ ★ DIFFICULTY: EASY 🍴 SERVINGS: 6-8

INGREDIENTS

For the Cream Layer
- 1 cup heavy cream or whipped coconut cream (chilled)
- ½ cup coconut milk (full-fat)
- 2 Tbsp sugar or honey
- ½ tsp vanilla extract
- Pinch of pa'akai (Hawaiian sea salt)

For the Fruit Layer
- 1 ripe mango, diced
- ½ ripe papaya, diced
- 1 Tbsp lime juice
- 1 Tbsp honey or agave
- Zest of ½ lime

For the Sponge Layer
- 12 ladyfinger cookies or slices of sponge cake
- ½ cup champagne or sparkling guava juice
- Optional: splash of rum or coconut liqueur (for an adult twist)

For Garnish
- Toasted coconut flakes
- Fresh mint sprigs
- Sliced mango or edible flowers (orchid, hibiscus, or bougainvillea)

INSTRUCTIONS

Prepare the Coconut Whip
1. In a chilled bowl, beat heavy cream or whipped coconut cream with sugar, coconut milk, vanilla, and a pinch of salt.
2. Whip until soft peaks form, light, glossy, and slightly airy.
3. Chill until ready to assemble.

Marinate the Fruit
1. Toss diced mango and papaya with lime juice, zest, and honey.
2. Let sit for 10–15 minutes to macerate and develop syrupy sweetness.

Assemble the Float
1. In a trifle bowl or small glasses, begin with a layer of sponge or ladyfingers.
2. Brush or drizzle with champagne (or sparkling guava) until lightly moistened.
3. Spoon a layer of macerated fruit, then a generous layer of coconut whip.
4. Repeat layers until you reach the top.
5. Finish with a final swirl of coconut whip and garnish with fruit and toasted coconut.

Chill & Serve
- Refrigerate for 2–3 hours before serving to let flavors meld and bubbles infuse.
- Serve cold, ideally just as the new year countdown begins, light, elegant, and joyfully tropical.

Tropical Fruit & Passion Fruit Sorbet "Countdown" Cups

CHEF'S NOTES

- Timing Tip: Make all components ahead, assemble just before serving for best texture contrast.
- Flavor Harmony: The tart lilikoi balances the sweet mango-pineapple perfectly, while the coconut whip adds creamy luxury.
- Color Story: Choose fruits with bold hues, yellow, pink, orange, for a layered "fireworks" presentation.
- Adult Twist: Add a drizzle of rum, sparkling wine, or pineapple liqueur for a cocktail-style dessert.
- Serving Style: Serve in coupe glasses or clear rocks glasses for that "midnight toast" aesthetic.

TASTING NOTES

- Aroma: Tropical and floral, fresh mango, coconut, and passion fruit perfume.
- Taste: Tangy-sweet balance with creamy coconut finish and bursts of juicy fruit.
- Texture: Silky sorbet melts into whipped coconut cream with pops of crisp fruit and toasted coconut.
- Color: Vibrant sunset shades, gold, coral, and white, a visual celebration of a Hawaiian New Year.

Tropical Fruit & Passion Fruit Sorbet "Countdown" Cups

A refreshing layered dessert of tropical fruit, tangy lilikoi (passion fruit) sorbet, and coconut sparkle, the perfect finale for New Year's in Hawai'i

 COOK TIME: 20 MINS   DIFFICULTY: EASY   SERVINGS: 6-8

INGREDIENTS

For the Sorbet (Lilikoi Layer)
- 1 cup fresh lilikoi (passion fruit) pulp (about 6–8 fruits)
- ½ cup sugar or honey
- ½ cup water
- 1 Tbsp lime juice
- Optional: splash of sparkling guava soda or champagne for adult version. (Or use high-quality store-bought passion fruit sorbet to save time.)

For the Tropical Fruit Mix
- ½ cup diced pineapple
- ½ cup diced mango
- ½ cup diced papaya
- ¼ cup sliced kiwi or lychee
- 1 Tbsp lime juice
- 1 Tbsp honey or agave
- Zest of ½ lime

For the Coconut Whip (Top Layer)
- 1 cup chilled coconut cream (from a can, solids only)
- 2 Tbsp powdered sugar or honey
- ½ tsp vanilla extract
- Pinch of pa'akai (Hawaiian sea salt)

For Garnish
- Toasted coconut flakes
- Edible flowers (orchid or hibiscus)
- Pomegranate arils or gold dust sugar for sparkle
- Fresh mint sprigs

INSTRUCTIONS

Make the Sorbet
1. In a small saucepan, combine sugar and water; heat until dissolved.
2. Cool, then mix with lilikoi pulp and lime juice.
3. Pour into an ice cream maker and churn according to manufacturer's directions, or freeze in a shallow dish, stirring every 30 minutes until set (2–3 hours).
4. For a festive twist, stir in a splash of sparkling guava just before serving.

Prepare the Fruit Mix
1. Combine pineapple, mango, papaya, kiwi, lime juice, honey, and zest.
2. Chill for at least 15 minutes to allow flavors to blend.

Make the Coconut Whip
1. Scoop chilled coconut cream solids into a mixing bowl.
2. Whip with sugar, vanilla, and salt until soft peaks form.
3. Keep refrigerated until ready to assemble.

Assemble the "Countdown" Cups
1. In clear glass cups or mini dessert bowls, add a spoonful of tropical fruit mixture.
2. Top with a scoop of lilikoi sorbet.
3. Add a small dollop of coconut whip.
4. Garnish with toasted coconut, mint, pomegranate, or edible flowers for sparkle.

Midnight Lilikoi Margarita
(or Non-Alcoholic Lilikoi Cooler)
CHEF'S NOTES

- Lilikoi Magic: Use fresh lilikoi pulp with seeds strained for a silky texture, or leave a few seeds for sparkle.
- Salt Rim: The combination of sugar and pa'akai enhances both tartness and fruit flavor, a signature Hawaiian touch.
- Batch It: Double or triple the recipe for parties; serve in a glass dispenser with frozen fruit cubes for flair.
- Variation: Add muddled basil or fresh pineapple for a layered tropical aroma.
- Presentation: Serve in coupe glasses for elegance or mason jars for casual luau style.

TASTING NOTES

- Aroma: Bright passion fruit, lime zest, and faint floral sweetness, tropical and effervescent.
- Taste: Perfect balance of tart, sweet, and salty with a citrusy pop and silky mouthfeel.
- Texture: Smooth, juicy, and lightly sparkling, the bubbles carry each note upward.
- Color: Sunset gold with a glimmer of lime, a toast to new beginnings.

Midnight Lilikoi Margarita
(or Non-Alcoholic Lilikoi Cooler)

A luminous passion fruit cocktail (or mocktail) kissed with lime, sea salt, and island sunshine, the perfect midnight toast in paradise

 COOK TIME: 10 MINS   DIFFICULTY: EASY   SERVINGS: 2-4

INGREDIENTS

For the Lilikoi Base
- ¾ cup fresh lilikoi (passion fruit) pulp or juice
- 2 Tbsp honey or agave syrup (to taste)
- 1 Tbsp lime juice
- Pinch of pa'akai (Hawaiian sea salt)

For the Margarita Version
- 3 oz silver tequila or reposado
- 1 oz orange liqueur (Cointreau or triple sec)
- 1 oz fresh lime juice
- Ice cubes
- Optional: splash of sparkling guava soda for lift

For the Non-Alcoholic Cooler
- ½ cup sparkling guava soda or club soda
- ½ cup chilled coconut water
- Extra squeeze of lime

For Garnish
- Pa'akai and sugar for rim
- Lime wheel or wedge
- Edible flower (orchid or hibiscus)
- Mint sprig or passion fruit seed float

INSTRUCTIONS

Prepare the Lilikoi Base
1. In a shaker or small jar, combine lilikoi pulp, honey, lime juice, and a pinch of salt.
2. Shake or whisk until honey dissolves completely.
3. Taste and adjust sweetness, it should balance tartness with a soft tropical finish.

For the Margarita (Alcoholic Version)
1. Rim glasses with a mix of pa'akai and sugar.
2. In a cocktail shaker filled with ice, combine 3 oz tequila, 1 oz orange liqueur, 1 oz lime juice, and 3 oz lilikoi base.
3. Shake vigorously until frosty.
4. Strain into prepared glasses over fresh ice.
5. Optional: top with a splash of sparkling guava soda for a festive effervescence.

For the Lilikoi Cooler (Non-Alcoholic Version)
1. Rim glasses with sugar or coconut flakes for a playful look.
2. In a shaker, mix 4 oz lilikoi base with ½ cup sparkling guava soda and ½ cup coconut water.
3. Stir gently (do not shake carbonated drinks).
4. Pour over ice and garnish with mint and lime.

BOOKS BY R.J. PICKRELL

COOKBOOK
Aloha in Every Bite: Volume 1

TAHA THE KAVA SERIES
Taha the Kava: Aloha New Friend!
COMING SOON
Taha and the Rainbow of Big Feelings
Taha and the Courage to Start Something New
Taha and the Friendship Mix Up
Taha and the Courage to Try

CHILDREN'S COLORING BOOK
Aloha Adventures: A Hawaiian Coloring Journey

HUMOR
Whiskered Words of Frisky Felines

SCIENCE FICTION
COMING SOON
Star Guardians: The Quest for Luminara

www.ingramcontent.com/pod-product-compliance
Lightning Source LLC
Chambersburg PA
CBRC091205010526
44107CB00021B/1253